T0328778

Cambridge Elements ≡

Elements in Beckett Studies
edited by
Dirk Van Hulle
University of Oxford
Mark Nixon
University of Reading

BAD *GODOTS:* '*VLADIMIR EMERGES FROM THE BARREL*' AND OTHER INTERVENTIONS

S. E. Gontarski
Florida State University

CAMBRIDGE
UNIVERSITY PRESS

CAMBRIDGE
UNIVERSITY PRESS

Shaftesbury Road, Cambridge CB2 8EA, United Kingdom

One Liberty Plaza, 20th Floor, New York, NY 10006, USA

477 Williamstown Road, Port Melbourne, VIC 3207, Australia

314–321, 3rd Floor, Plot 3, Splendor Forum, Jasola District Centre,
New Delhi – 110025, India

103 Penang Road, #05–06/07, Visioncrest Commercial, Singapore 238467

Cambridge University Press is part of Cambridge University Press & Assessment,
a department of the University of Cambridge.

We share the University's mission to contribute to society through the pursuit of
education, learning and research at the highest international levels of excellence.

www.cambridge.org
Information on this title: www.cambridge.org/9781009467803

DOI: 10.1017/9781009180702

First published 2024

A catalogue record for this publication is available from the British Library

ISBN 978-1-009-46780-3 Hardback
ISBN 978-1-009-18071-9 Paperback
ISSN 2632-0746 (online)
ISSN 2632-0738 (print)

Bad *Godots*

'Vladimir Emerges from the Barrel' and other Interventions

Elements in Beckett Studies

DOI: 10.1017/9781009180702
First published online: January 2024

S. E. Gontarski
Florida State University
Author for correspondence: S. E. Gontarski, sgontarski@fsu.edu

Abstract: This Element focuses on the machinery of commercial theatre, on extra-authorial interventions into the creative process and on the people and institutional forces that foster them. Such a process challenges the autonomy of the artwork and authorial integrity. The primary focus of this Element is then on the hybrid genre of theatre where collective esthetics tends to override and so to supersede individual creation. The essay pays special attention to Samuel Beckett's first professionally produced play, *Waiting for Godot*, primarily its English language premieres in the US, UK, and the Republic of Ireland. Its implications, however, reach far beyond the genetic and production histories of a single theatrical work to deal with the nature of authorship in a monetized culture, the process of realizing dramatic texts in such a culture, and Samuel Beckett's engagement with such machinery of art.

This Element also has a video abstract:
www.cambridge.org/Gontarski-BadGodots

Keywords: co-authorship, textual reliability, theatrical adaptation, commercial art and monetary culture, publication history

ISBNs: 9781009467803 (HB), 9781009180719 (PB), 9781009180702 (OC)
ISSNs: 2632-0746 (online), 2632-0738 (print)

Contents

1 Overview: A Genealogy of Intervention

Samuel Beckett was something of an accidental dramatist, or at least his earliest completed plays were written almost as a sideline, a diversion from the long narrative flights he was developing in a white heat in the aftermath of the Second World War, the trio of breakthrough French novels now loosely called *The Trilogy*. Theatre, he would subsequently say, was 'a relaxation from the awful prose I was writing at that time'; it offered an escape from 'the wildness and rulelessness of the novels', and he would call it 'a marvelous, liberating diversion' because of its plasticity, its concreteness, its thereness, particular people (more or less) in particular spaces (more or less) (Beckett qtd in Cronin, 1997, 390). He could not have anticipated how thoroughly these diversions, these exercises in creative relaxation, his dabbling in the most public and collaborative of the literary arts, a hybrid genre between a necessarily incomplete script and its performative, commercial realisation, would force him, uncomfortably at first, into a public sphere. The inevitable transition from an artist's private production to the commodity-driven economics of performance would come to violate what he tended to call, his legacy from James Joyce, perhaps, 'artistic integrity', his perceived creative autonomy. Theatre's collaborative nature, on the other hand, invites, indeed relies on a division of labour, serial creative interventions, and more overt alliances with commerce than either the narrative or the lyrical arts, the path to theatrical realisation suggesting, as well, something of theatre's instability, fragility, and vulnerability. Theatre, an afterthought in the late 1940s, would grow to dominate Beckett's creative life. While the Nobel Prize committee announced its award to Samuel Beckett on 24 October 1969 for his writing 'in new forms for the novel and drama',[1] he is designated as a 'playwright' in *The Times* announcement: 'The Irish-born playwright Samuel Beckett [is] acknowledged as one of the greatest living dramatists for his pioneering new modes of theatrical expression' (qtd in Faber, 2019, 303).

When *En attendant Godot* (*Waiting for Godot*), the second of these creative diversions or exercises in relaxation, finally premiered in Paris at the Théâtre de Babylone on 5 January 1953, the 47-year-old debutant playwright had been a full-time writer and translator for some 23 years. He published his first separate piece, the long poem *Whoroscope*, in 1930, which he wrote in several hours on 15 June for a contest on the subject of time sponsored by Richard Aldington and Nancy Cunard. The poem ridiculed the personal peccadillos of the philosopher René Descartes (1596–1650) and, with its awkward, intrusive

---

[1] The Nobel Prize in Literature 1969. NobelPrize.org. Nobel Prize Outreach AB 2021. Saturday, 24 July 2021. www.nobelprize.org/prizes/literature/1969/summary/

footnotes, laid waste to T. S. Eliot's landmark, cut-up mosaic of Western decline, *The Waste Land*; it won first prize. Soon after *Godot*'s modest Parisian success and its subsequent European tour, Beckett began to translate the play into English in response to interest from an American publisher and London and New York producers. Despite the difficulties of placing his early English fiction, *Dream of Fair to Middling Women* (segmented or cut up into *More Pricks than Kicks*), *Murphy*, and *Watt*, with publishers (economic issues, mostly), and their subsequent banning in his native Ireland (political issues, mostly), Beckett seemed less fully aware of the politics of art and the interface of art and commerce than one might expect given that his initial full-length excursion into drama, the still-unproduced *Eleutheria*, mocked what Adorno and Horkheimer would call *The Culture Industry*. *Eleutheria* would travesty the conventions of commercial, boulevard entertainments and posit an overt counter-commitment to bohemianism and so to decadence. That is, in Beckett's dealings with production, he seems not to have comprehended fully the move from creation as private labour to art as a product of multiple social forces or, that is, the degree to which theatre production entailed commodity production, art as a product mediated by a market, although he was savvy enough to warn his French publisher of 'this adaptation business' as requests for English-language performance rights began to arrive in Paris in 1953 (Beckett, 2011, 379; qtd in Van Hulle and Verhulst, 2018, 267). He did, however, speak with Michel Polac on Radiodiffusion Française in February 1952, that is, on the eve of his overt involvement in theatre, on the issue of art and commerce. Beckett's comments were designed as something of an introduction to a reading of extracts from *En attendant Godot*, almost a year before the play officially opened in Paris, and he was asked specifically for his ideas about theatre. He began as follows: 'I have no ideas about theatre. I know nothing about it. I do not go to it'; but he did follow with a prescient insight into the performance contradiction: 'It is not given to everyone to be able to move from the world that opens under the page to that of profit and loss then back again, unperturbed, as if between the daily grind and the pub on the corner'. This was the world he was on the threshold of entering, and he was aware as well, at least in the abstract, that he was about to lose control of his product, and willingly so, at least at this point: 'I am no longer part of it, and never will be again. [. . .] Let them get on with it. Without me. They and I have settled our accounts' (Beckett, 2011, 316).

While the French staging of *Godot* was plagued by economic delays, political infighting, and the author's reluctance to let go of his product, or at least to turn full control over to others and declare his 'accounts' with this new work 'settled', the path to English production and subsequent publication was littered with forced divestment, with various curiosities emerging through the process, including altered scripts, competing translations, cultural prohibitions, various interventions, and other struggles for creative control that seem to have caught Beckett unawares as he struggled to maintain some level of artistic integrity for his vision of humanity in decline, something of an atavistic comedy, what we today might call dystopian modernism. Such a vision of human regression is articulated (if that is the word) by a former intellectual now menial artist-figure, tied (literally) to an economic power, displayed for entertainment purposes, and finally offered as an object for sale, Lucky. Beckett's dealings with the insular coteries of the Paris avant-garde, which were not without their own economic issues and political conflicts, were poor preparation for the adepts, the businessmen and businesswomen of the Anglo-American theatre world, the American agents Marion Saunders and Georges Borchardt, the British literary agents Curtis Brown and Rosica Colin, and producers of Broadway and the West End, namely Peter Glenville and Harold Oram (who dropped out early), Donald Albery, and the American impresario Michael Myerberg. They would all treat the originating artist with suspicion, as unnecessary for their purposes, an encumbrance almost, even an impediment to the work's full and final realisation. Responding to Howard Turner, the publisher Barney Rosset's office assistant, on 2 August 1955, on the eve of the London opening of *Waiting for Godot*, Beckett assessed his creative isolation:

> I am not very optimistic about the Arts Theatre production, though I have not much to go on. The London people have treated me with studied unfriendliness from the outset, leaving me in the dark as to their intentions (never the same two weeks running) and not consulting me at any stage about cast, setting and production generally. I suppose the payment of what may be regarded as a handsome advance on royalties entitles them to all extremes of offhandedness. I shall not go over for the opening. I think their intention is to run until the end of this month only [August 1955]. I surmise this production is in the nature of a try-out in place of the usual try-out in the provinces and that, if the play is well received, it will be transferred to a larger theatre. But this again is just my own idea, based on nothing more tangible than the assumption that [producer Donald] Albery would like his money back, and perhaps even a little over. (letter not included in *The Letters of Samuel Beckett*; see SULSC, Box 104)[2]

---

[2] Letters for this period between Samuel Beckett and Barney Rosset (and other employees at Grove Press) are found in and available at Grove Press Records, Special Collections Research Center, Syracuse University Libraries, cited hereafter as SULSC. In particular, the Beckett–Rosset correspondence on *Waiting for Godot* of this period is available in Box 104, *Waiting for Godot*, 'Correspondence 1953–1969' and 'Correspondence, re: Michael Myerberg 1955–1956, 1962, 1966–1969'. In 2010 and 2014, Columbia University purchased the Barney Rosset Papers, now in the Rare Book and Manuscript Library, Columbia University Library, and substantial portions

Beckett wrote almost an identical assessment a few days later, 18 August 1955, to Pamela Mitchell, who for a time represented Harold Oram:

> I think, though I don't know, not having been told, that the Arts production is in the nature of a try-out (in place of the pre-westend provincial tour) and that the play may be transferred to a larger theatre later on, this ingenuous theory being based on nothing more serious than the assumption that Albery and Co. would like to get their money back and if possible a little over. They have been markedly unfriendly to me throughout, leaving me in the dark as to their plans and not consulting me at any stage, though their contract specifies they must, about cast, settings and so on. (Beckett, 2011, 539–40)

Writing to Rosset on 19 April 1956, Beckett recounted his continued isolated status, now from several *Godot* productions, especially, at this stage, from business and financial matters:

> Not a fluke so far from Saunders or Colin, I think it's against their principles. No news from Pike [Theatre in Dublin] either, though they should have by now lodged my royalties with my Dublin bank and sent you your whack. I don't want to chivvy them yet a while. No news from Albery whose production should be touring or preparing to tour the provinces. (letter not included in *The Letters of Samuel Beckett*; see SULSC, Box 104)

Beckett's French theatrical experience was quite the opposite, as Van Hulle and Verhulst report: 'He spent much of the following months [of late 1952] working with director Roger Blin and the actors, during which he made considerable changes to the text of the first edition in his personal "prompt copy"' (Van Hulle and Verhulst, 2018, 80–1).

Such issues of keeping the author at bay in the commercial theatres of Britain and the United States have a particular irony given that a central feature of what had become Beckett's first produced play was the enslavement and monetisation of an artist/intellectual/teacher/performer by an overlord/businessman who in Act I was in the process of leading his now-damaged commodity to market for sale ('Guess who taught me all these beautiful things. [...] My Lucky';

overlap the Syracuse collection: https://findingaids.library.columbia.edu/ead/nnc-rb/ldpd_7953908/dsc/6#subseries_1.

The author has worked with material from Barney Rosset's personal archive since 1985. In May 2013, the author's Rosset and Grove Press material was transferred to and is currently available at Florida State University (FSU), which also includes material related to the 'Beckett–Rosset Correspondence' project prepared for Faber and Faber with the cooperation and approval of the Beckett and Rosset estates. The analysis here draws on that material as well: FSU Special Collections & Archives / MSS 2013-0516, Stanley E. Gontarski Grove Press Research Materials / Literary Manuscripts, Box: 10, Folder: 1: https://archives.lib.fsu.edu/subjects/2364.

Some of the 'previously unpublished' letters cited in this study have appeared and have been cited in Gontarski (2011, 374–82). All previously unpublished letters are currently reproduced with the permission of Edward Beckett and the Samuel Beckett and the Rosset estates.

Beckett, 1954, 22), although in the play's visual imagery it is Pozzo who is being led. The producers and other adepts of the Anglo-American theatrical world would take it upon themselves, blatantly at times, to reshape the work of a neophyte playwright to increase the product's accessibility, and so its monetary value, even as Beckett's creative thrust continued single-mindedly towards a counter goal, the development of what would become his Dystopian Trilogy, *Godot*, *Endgame*, and *Happy Days*, something of a theatrical cluster featuring human and environmental decline, what Estragon calls a 'muckheap', or a 'landscape' dominated by 'worms' (Beckett, 1954, 39b) in Act II of *Godot* after Lucky's prophetic pronouncement in Act I that humanity 'wastes and pines' (29). Such visible signs of degradation, then, parallel the ontological dispersal amid Beckett's post-war sequence of French novels.

But the process, the machinery of theatrical production and the economic forces that drive it, stands, as well, as testimony to Beckett's artistic resilience. As he wrangled with and became entangled by the forces that constitute theatre and commerce, or theatre as commerce, say, he would evolve into his own interventionist, staging his plays and, like other interventionists, rewriting or reshaping them in the process of their realisation, their spatial articulation, revalidating thereby an aesthetics of serial process, excising whatever he deemed untheatrical clutter, and so sharpening the outlines of his vision. Such a preoccupation ran counter to that of Beckett's commercial handlers who constantly engaged in attempts to fill theatrical gaps as if those perceived absences reflected creative deficiencies. Beckett's own intervention into his first dramatic success was the result of his accepting an invitation from Berlin's Schiller Theater in 1975. In Berlin, he was part of a system where the writer was included in the theatrical process. He could thus limit interventions into the artwork by others, and he could work outside the usual economic strictures of fully commercial theatre. He would return to stage that play in English in 1984, directing, or at least overseeing, a production with the American actor Rick Cluchey at the Riverside Studios, London.[3] Beckett's London participation was essentially a favour to the actor who headed the San Quentin Drama Workshop. In September 1988, Beckett gifted copies of the textual and theatrical revisions for both Berlin (1975) and London (1984) productions to Cluchey, and since 1 July 2014 those documents have been

---

[3] See Beckett's structural outline of the play: https://samuelbeckettsociety.org/2017/12/08/beck ett-annotated-godot/ . See also 'Manuscript Annotations by Samuel Beckett in a Copy of *Waiting for Godot* for a Production by the San Quentin Drama Workshop': www.bl.uk/collection-items/ manuscript-annotations-by-samuel-beckett-in-a-copy-of-waiting-for-godot-for-a-production- by-the-san-quentin-drama-workshop.

archived at Washington University, St. Louis. The archivist's note on these
performance revisions offers the following overview:

> Beckett had long believed the play to be confusing [actually not] and clumsily
> visualized [only somewhat], though, and he used the opportunity his direct-
> orial debut [actually not] provided to clarify both the text and stage directions.
> Copiously marked up with colored underlining and autograph notations, the
> book reveals in vivid detail the extensive revisions Beckett made to his
> original work, which included dialogue changes, the excision of entire
> scenes, new directorial emphases, and alterations to the staging. (WU, Rick
> Cluchey Collection of *Waiting for Godot* Materials, Box VMF 20, folder 4)[4]

Beckett's interventions, however, his emendations, say, tended not to be commodity-driven, nor to have much to do with commerce at all. With the initial
Waiting for Godot experience, however, he was drawn deeper into such commerce, the economics, the business of art production, and he began to function
less as an author working in isolation than as a company manager, the CEO,
perhaps, of Beckett Enterprises, as he negotiated salaries, royalties, and other
emoluments, engaged in quality control, headed product research and development, and engaged, to some extent, in community relations. Barney Rosset in
turn would function as Beckett's CFO, keeping him apprised and so involved in
the economics of art production and management, even as Beckett, on occasion,
tried to distance himself from those roles.

  Collectively, these economic, political, and aesthetic processes that intersect
theatrical production form their own archaeological mosaic, a set of often material curiosities that details not only Beckett's developing theatrical art but the
process of art, particularly commercial theatrical production in a monetised,
commodity-driven culture often called late capitalism. T. S. Eliot could embrace
what he saw as creative intervention in the rearrangement and reshaping of his
poetic, cut-up mosaic or collage, and he would celebrate the interventionist, Ezra
Pound, as the *better* craftsman. But Pound's interventions were done openly.

---

[4] 'Rick Cluchey Collection of *Waiting for Godot* Materials, 1954–1965'. Washington University
Libraries (cited hereafter as WU), Department of Special Collections (https://aspace.wustl.edu/
repositories/6/resources/607/collection_organization). This is one of four texts revised by Beckett
for performance, two for the Schiller production in 1975 and two for Riverside in 1984. Beckett
had also given a photocopy of the Cluchey text to the University of Reading Beckett Archive, and
it, along with the three other revised copies of *Godot*, forms the core of the text of *Waiting for
Godot* that James Knowlson, with Dougald MacMillan, used to establish the final revised acting
text that appears in *The Theatrical Notebooks of Samuel Beckett* (Beckett, 1994). All the revised
texts are available in that volume in facsimile, transcription, and translation. Cluchey's '2nd
prompt book' used for the Riverside production is also on deposit at Washington University, but
this document was not consulted for the *Godot Theatrical Notebook* (Van Hulle and Verhulst,
2018, 162–3). Another copy is on deposit at DePaul University (Van Hulle and Verhulst, 2018,
165) and one remains in private hands (163).

Beckett, on the other hand, would try to resist such intervention as best he could, but he was often overwhelmed by the invisible machinery of art and the matrix of cultural forces that, finally, throw into question the integrity and autonomy of authorship since changes, revisions, and adjustments were often made by stealth, that is, without authorial knowledge or approval. Commercial theatre, Beckett would find, was an economic machine through which private labour was transformed and the author/labourer at times marginalised or alienated as additional labour entered the process of commodity production, the entire machine designed to generate surplus value for investors even as art appeared to maintain its distance from the utilitarian and the material. It is pertinent to recall, for example, that in his *Aesthetic Theory* Theodor Adorno called art the 'absolute commodity', or more fully, 'The absolute artwork converges with the absolute commodity' (Adorno qtd in Suther, 2017, 104). Jensen Suther summarises the critic Stewart Martin on such convergence:

> For Martin, this striking claim is key to understanding Adorno's theory of modernism, and explodes the antinomy between two contemporary, countervailing aesthetic theories, one that insists that the work of art is, as a commodity, insuperably determined by capital, and one that claims that the artwork is autonomous and insulated from the process of exchange. (Martin qtd in Suther, 2017, 104–5; see also Martin, 2007, 18)

In Martin's terms,

> autonomous art effectively comes into being with commodification, which frees certain products from their heteronomous determination by the church, state or other forms of patronage, and, through the indeterminacy of their ultimate buyer, such works acquire an independent sense of their end and value. Autonomous art is thus an ornament of capitalist culture. On the other hand, there is the position that autonomous art is destroyed by developed capitalism. According to this view, the development of commodification as a general principle of society reduces all values to exchange-value, including the value of art, and thereby destroys art's autonomy. Capitalist culture is consequently the death of autonomous art. (Martin, 2007, 16)

Such curiosities detailed herein offer an alternate genealogy of the 'antimony' between or the convergence of art and commodity, or at least of their unstable and shifting alliances, as Martin details in the quote above, not only, that is, of a single work per se but of a cultural process, the machinery of commodity-driven art competing in a marketplace with other commodities, an object for investment with an expectation of a greater return, and so they alter an artistic and critical landscape in terms of the interface of private labour, commodity economics, and the generation of surplus value through artefacts displayed for sale to an anonymous public. Beckett seems to have wanted it both ways: the integrity of the individually produced, autonomous artwork, on the one hand, and the rewards of communally produced commodity production and sale, on the other. In this regard, we might argue that Beckett's challenge was close to that of Marx and part of the 'dissonance' that Adorno saw as inherent to modernism, at least as summarised by Suther:

> The artwork conceals its social determination and origin in the division of labor and does so precisely as a commodity, in accord with the logic of commodity fetishism. Because, however, the work insists on its autonomy from any external end, it mobilizes fetishism against its own commodification. In this way, as Martin argues, the exchange value of the artwork is the only possible value. (Suther, 2017, 107)

The initial stagings of *Waiting for Godot*, American, British, and Irish, constituted Beckett's full immersion into the Anglo-American theatre business, and once entering the process, his entanglement in the machinery of commercial art production with its economic balance sheets, he very quickly lost creative autonomy as his literature of dissonance, as Adorno might have called it, was appropriated and capitalised. He would spend the remainder of his creative life recovering, struggling to re-establish the autonomy of his artworks in a marketplace, and much of his strategy was not only to restrict interventions contractually, that is, to turn the machinery of commercial theatrical production back on itself, but to become his own interventionist. The process that generated his own productions and their inevitable self-interventions was in part an attempt to resolve the tensions between the artwork as autonomous 'from any external end', with its aesthetics of dissonance, and the collaborative aesthetics and monetised demands that constitute commercial theatre.

2 Broadway and other Theatrical Adepts

On 4 November 1954, the American publisher Barney Rosset informed his new author that

> [the American producer Michael] Myerberg informs me that *Godot* is due to open, providing that contracts get signed, in Miami, Florida on January 3rd [1956] and then make two additional stops en route to New York. This all sounds very wonderful and I will keep my fingers crossed until all arrangements are completed. If all goes well I will print a new edition of the play, to look like the old one excepting that it will be done with a paper jacket and will sell for something like $1.00. (Rosset, 2017, 92)

As production neared the following year, 22 November 1955, Beckett had got word that the American playwright Thornton Wilder was involved with the American staging of *Godot* and wrote to the play's newly named American director, Alan Schneider: 'I hear there was talk in your papers of Wilder coming to our rescue with an adaptation of my play. This would make me laugh if it was not prohibited' (Beckett, 2011, 574). The American premiere had from the outset been cloaked in secrecy, dogged by rumour, marked by confusion and commercial machinations, and on 29 November 1955, Rosset laid out his frustrations about his being left out of theatrical planning, and, as owner of world performance rights, he focused on the business end of theatre and publishing:

> Myerberg, whom I have still not met, and who has still not presented any written contracts, is supposed to give me a go-ahead signal for a new edition of *Godot*. I now have in all my printing estimates and I would be very happy to go ahead with a paperbound edition to sell for $1.00. The time is getting very short and I have constantly pressed the producer to settle final details. This aspect of things bothers me a little, but perhaps next week will see it all cleared up. If we do this edition, and if *Godot* survives the New York winter, I am sure we could do quite nicely with it, in the theater alone. This would also mean more immediate income for you. I received a nice note from Albery, but although I receive constant reassurances from everybody, including [the French publisher Jérôme] Lindon, I have not yet seen hide nor hair of anything in writing about the New York production. Lindon, in a letter, agreed to let me have the same 10 percent of his share for the New York production as for the London one and Myerberg, over the phone, more than agreed in respect to that agreement. However I am getting more cynical as the years go by and I want Mr. Myerberg to put it in writing. [These business details appear in a dictated draft signed thus, BR/sr, but they were edited out of the signed facsimile letter that is published in Rosset, 2017, 95. Both versions are available at SULSC, Box 104.]

On 6 December 1955, with *Waiting for Godot* scheduled to open in Coral Gables, Florida within a month and rehearsals well under way, Rosset sounded a full alarm to his new author on the issue of textual fidelity:

> A moment ago a man walked in here [to the Grove Press New York offices] who wants to put on a special showing of *Godot* for agents, actors, etc.
> This fellow informed me that he had seen a statement in the newspapers to the effect that Thornton Wilder was going to write an adaptation of your play and that would be the one to be put on Broadway. [...] It certainly annoys hell [*sic*] out of me and my first reaction is to say – let Mr. Wilder write his own play, talented as he may be, and let yours go on a la Beckett [*sic*]. (Rosset, 2017, 98)

Tensions between the American publisher and the play's American producer tended to run high, and Rosset complained further to Beckett about financial arrangements (since both, finally, were now part of the culture industry) the following day, 7 December 1955, in the process drawing him further into the business of production:

> Believe me, I want to do what you want, but why in God's name must it be you who has to guarantee me something, and not the people who take in the money at the box office. If everybody agrees on everything, why cannot this Myerberg put something into writing. I am not a mad ogre waiting here to gobble him up. In fact the opposite has been true – I have tried to help him in any possible [way], and what is most important, I have been waiting for him to give me the go ahead signal on putting out the paperbound edition of *Godot* – at <u>my</u> expense, and he has not even come through on that. He said the new edition should have a new photo on the cover, using the American actors. That seemed perfectly reasonable to me, but no photograph has ever been forthcoming.
>
> Myerberg disturbed me when he said that the English version of the play [already revised by Beckett and in print by Grove since autumn 1954] was not well translated, and that disturbance was heightened when I was told about the Wilder story in the paper (he to do an adaptation) but I infer from your cable that all is okay along those lines.
>
> I do appreciate your cable of assurance, and you can know that I want to do as you desire. (Rosset, 2017, 102)

While in a letter dated 18 June 1953 (published in facsimile), Rosset could offer Beckett some good news as the constant ebb and flow of information fluctuated wildly, the typed date of 18 June 1953 is here confusing, since Rosset wrote Beckett on 28 December 1955 that 'the printing order has been given for the $1.00 edition of Godot' [*sic*] (Rosset, 2017, 105). More likely the letter below is from June 1955: in June 1953, Rosset was still addressing his new author as 'Mr Beckett' (62):

> This morning two GOOD developments. First, I got sick of waiting for Myerberg to tell me that everything was really set and I gave the printer orders to proceed with a new edition of *Godot*, to sell at $1.00. I hope this please [*sic*] you. If Myerberg does not come through with a new photograph I will simply use the existing jacket [with photos Beckett had suggested] which I like anyway [see also Rosset, 2016, 120].
>
> Secondly, yesterday's letter to Myerberg finally produced results. His attorney called my attorney this morning and apparently they had a long and agreeable conversation. It ended by Moselle's (Myerberg's atty.) saying that he would produce all the information we want by the end of next week, and it seems that after that we should be able to make an agreement. My fingers are crossed. [. . .] I am only swearing at myself for delaying so long in activating the new [paperback] edition of *Godot*.[5] (Rosset, 2017, 100)

---

[5] Rosset's eagerness to publish was driven in good part by robust book sales: 'The publishing house had sold out its original $4.75 edition of the play. In February, *Waiting for Godot* appeared in a $1.00 paperback, and its first printing of five-thousand copies *sold out before publication*' (Levy, 1956, 35; emphasis added). Rosset's numbers are more modest, as he reported to Beckett

What Rosset did not know on the eve of the Miami opening was that Wilder had completely redrafted Beckett's translation, and, presumably, then, the *Godot* that audiences would see in Miami and subsequently in New York would be considerably different, at least more Americanised, than the text that Rosset had been selling for a year and would now reissue in paperback in conjunction with the anticipated New York opening. But with the prospect of printed and performed texts differing substantially, such disparity might have needed notification, at least a programme acknowledgement, the Broadway adept given official credit, the stage version now deemed co-authored, perhaps, or at least co-translated if the Wilder alterations, or, as it turned out, the Wilder–Schneider revisions were those staged. The New York theatre *Playbill* might need to acknowledge 'Book by Thornton Wilder', a practice not uncommon on the Broadway stage, or 'Additional dialogue by Thornton Wilder'.

On 25 October 1955, moreover, Rosset had informed Beckett that one English-language script of *Godot* had already been altered and that Grove Press was now being billed for those changes. The expenses were apparently first passed on from Albery to Lindon, who in turn, since these involved the English-language text, was now passing them on to the agent who controlled North American publication but English-language performance rights, and Rosset kept Beckett informed on these and other financial details:

> I seem to have upset Albery by a letter to him, but do not let him upset you. I told him that I had to give permission for performances in English, but that obviously this was [now] after the fact ... my real object being to enforce my agreement with Lindon whereby I get 10% of gross received, to be taken out of Lindon's share. Lindon now confirms that and says he is so far holding 45 pounds for me. *He then goes on to say that revisions in the script were made and the cost of the revisions must come from my share.* (see SULSC, Box 104; emphasis added)

Lindon here is presumably referring to the ongoing and protracted negotiations between Albery and the Lord Chamberlain who had demanded script revisions before authorising a London West End production licence. Rosset was apparently reasserting to Albery his contractual arrangements with the Marion Saunders Literary Agency, the agreement signed on 19 June 1953. Point 2 plainly states: 'Grove Press will fully own this translation, and any book publisher, magazine publisher, play, radio, movie or television producer, etc., *in any country*, wanting to use that translation, will have to apply to Grove Press for permission', for which translation Beckett was paid $150 outright (Rosset, 2017, 60; emphasis added).

---

on 26 November 1955, 'Through October we had sold 406 copies of *Godot* [in hard back] and 544 copies of *Molloy*'. (These details as above edited out of the letter published in Rosset, 2017, 95.)

Rosset would subsequently acknowledge receiving Beckett's typescript translation and what must have been a professionally duplicated mimeographed copy of that original translation from Harold Oram on 31 July 1953 (Rosset, 2017, 67), so 'that translation' cited in the contract with Saunders presumably refers to Beckett's first typescript and Oram's subsequent mimeographed copy with its authorised and unauthorised revisions. The contract with Saunders/Lindon, then, would also cover Beckett's subsequent revised typescript, which Grove would eventually publish in autumn 1954, delayed at Beckett's request from spring. Beckett's response to Rosset on 26 October makes no mention of said 'revisions', however, but clarifies the economic relationship between Albery and Grove Press, affirming the latter as the 'proprietor of translation':

> You may rest assured that whatever moneys are due to you from here as proprietor of translation will be duly accounted for. [...] Albery seems to have got the idea you are contesting his rights. For heaven's sake write and tell him this is not so. (see SULSC, Box 104)

These rights had been in contention for years before the Miami, New York, or London openings. As early as 19 October 1953, Oram still in play as a producer, Rosset was summoned to the Marion Saunders offices, and, as Rosset recounts the story to Beckett, 'due to me the New York production had not proceeded. Somehow this was because I have a letter contract with you [...] which necessitates my approval of New York production' (Rosset, 2017, 70). Some of the issue was money, of course, as Rosset was requesting 1 per cent 'of the proceeds', net presumably. More important, perhaps, is Rosset's assurance that his approval would essentially be automatic if Saunders approved a production but with a proviso of fidelity to Beckett's text: 'My only concern would be to be sure that any cuts, changes or additions to the script were passed upon and approved by you' (Rosset, 2017, 70). That proviso would be substantially violated in the United States by November–December 1955.

Once the Grove paperback was released, it included a 'Caution' to clarify and specify rights to all English-language performances worldwide, but with an important stipulation as amateur groups seem to have been directed towards texts other than Grove's:

> All rights including professional, amateur, motion picture, radio, television, recitation, public reading, and any method of photographic reproduction, are strictly reserved. For amateur rights, apply to Dramatist Play Service, Inc. [...]. For stock rights, apply to Samuel French, Inc. [...]. For all other rights apply to Grove Press.

On 30 January 1957, Rosset's assistant for rights, Judith Schmidt, informed Beckett that 'Many amateur groups have written to us about *Godot* these past months and several are planning to produce the play. We're trying to get reports from them when it is possible' (see SULSC, Box 104). Such performance demand as Schmidt reports would trigger a new text, one designed specifically for amateur and 'stock' performance. By 1957, Samuel French, Inc. would begin to sell its own text, with its own statement of licensing rights that includes all 'performance of this play by amateurs'. In this process of granting amateur performance rights, Samuel French would naturally privilege its own, separately published but, as it turns out, altered and corrupt 'Acting Edition' of the play, which it sold throughout North America, the United Kingdom, and former Commonwealth countries, and in some areas through its own bookshops (two in the Los Angeles, California area, for instance, and one at London's Royal Court Theatre for a time). The phrase 'Acting Edition' carries with it a certain cachet, at least the implication or connotation is of an 'Authorised', 'Specialised', or even a 'Preferred Performance Script'. That 'Acting Edition' follows the Samuel French publication template by including all the expected performance niceties like a suggested set design, props, and lighting plot. For its *Godot* staging, French's 'Acting Edition' suggests, for example, a 'tree stump' and 'a rostrum' above 'stage level', the design used in London and imitated, to some extent, by Schneider in Miami. Props include a 'Tar barrel' as the first item, and Estragon's stated need for 'a good bit of rope' (Beckett, 1957, 60) is represented amid the props as 'string' for Vladimir and 'thin string as belt' for Estragon (Beckett, 1957, 72). The 'Lighting Plot' notes that the 'Main Acting Areas' are to be not only 'at a mound C' but 'at a barrel LC' (71 unpaginated), which is pictured in the drawing (70 unpaginated).

Beckett's American Collaborators

The plays Wilder saw in London and Paris and read in the Grove Press edition (the one perhaps colouring the other, depending on which came first) were considerably, even substantially different texts. To a large extent, such differences were generated by the machinery of commercial theatre. In the mid-1950s, a number of different English-language versions of Beckett's play were in simultaneous circulation among producers and actors, reproduced in different typings by stenographic and transcription services,[6] and those reproduced versions often bore fingerprints other than Beckett's. Peter Hall worked originally from mimeographed copies of Beckett's early (1953) translation since no British text was in print throughout *Godot*'s two London runs (Arts Theatre,

---

[6] Beckett was aware of the technology of textual reproduction in the theatre world of the time. He wrote to Rosset on 30 August 1957, '*Fin de Partie* or whatever it is called has been roneotyped and submitted to [Théâtre] Hébertot. We do not think he will take it' (Beckett, 2014, 647). In another letter to Rosset on 8 April 1959, Beckett said of the then unpublished *Premier Amour*, 'Bosquet asked me for an inédit to have polycopied and used in his class' (SULSC, Box 104).

August 1955; Criterion Theatre from 12 September 1955 to 24 March 1956), although the Grove Press edition had been available for a year, since 8 September 1954. Schneider also worked with a professionally retyped, customised version of the play in Miami, a practice not unusual in theatre (see, for example, Van Hulle and Verhulst, 2018, 159). The pages of Schneider's retyped promptbook include holes for brass clips or some sort of fasteners, the typed pages interlineated with blank sheets for notes, and its stage directions were typed in red to separate them at a glance, visually, from the dialogue.[7] Schneider, it turns out, would alter this script substantially. The actors for the Miami production most probably worked with carbon copies of this typescript. Schneider's copy then includes frequent dialogue rewrites, backstory details, as well as blocking notes for the ill-fated 1956 opening, even as the Grove Press text was readily available when Schneider began to collaborate with Wilder and when rehearsals began. The director took what we now consider substantial liberties with the version of the play he had, intervening freely, often following Wilder's lead to introduce frequent changes in phrasing, creating in the process an Americanised text. The promptbook also contains frequent drawings of a set so that the director could block character movements amid substantial dialogue alternatives. Schneider's set drawings are kidney-shaped, in part following Peter Snow's London design, and some of his notes are attempts to create something of a theatrical credibility for this story. He divides the action between 'Take time / Take space'. Under the rubric 'Take time', he notes, 'Struggle here on going / to get boot (shoe) off'. Following Wilder, Beckett's boots became shoes for Miami, the change indicated on the first page of the Wilder rewrite (Beckett, 1954, 7), but Beckett apparently slipped once as well and used 'shoe' in his original translation, and that was duplicated in all mimeographed copies (Beckett, 1953d, 1–43; Beckett, 1953a, b and c, 1–33; corrected in the published Grove text, Beckett, 1954, 24b). Under the rubric space, although undesignated as such, Schneider notes: 'Play Vladimir looking around a bit to get bearings' (Schneider, 1955, 4). To Beckett's 'Enter Vladimir', Schneider adds in brackets, by way of subtext, perhaps, 'From the john', a note transferred from the Wilderised copy, where 'john?' is lightly pencilled (Beckett, 1954, 7).

---

[7] The Schneider prompt book, as well as the bulk of his papers, is available at the University of California – San Diego (hereafter UCSD) Special Collections, Alan Schneider Papers, Call #: MSS 0103, promptbook in Box 11. Schneider's copy is a typed version (not a mimeograph) with the stage directions typed in red. It was evidently, given the nature of the paper, typed against several carbon copies, presumably for distribution to the actors. This text differs considerably from the mimeographed text that Donald Albery submitted to the Lord Chamberlain's office for approval and which Harold Oram or Michael Myerberg had retyped in New York (see Figure 3 in Section 5). My thanks to Heather Smedberg, Reference & Instruction Coordinator, Special Collections & Archives, UC San Diego Library, Mandeville Special Collections | Scripps Archives for making copies of the Schneider material available.

At the top of his promptbook Schneider lays out one pattern that he will try to follow, 'Elements of the city? / the country?'. His subsequent note, 'From the john', was evidently a 'city' designation to add something of an urban rehearsal or metatheatrical 'element' to the action (Schneider, 1955, 1–1) and to justify, to the actors at least, Estragon's comment, 'At the end of the corridor, on the left', but it punctuates as well Schneider's persistent attempts to create a credible subtext or backstory for his actors and finally for his audience. In the Wilder retranslation, in response to Beckett's 'And they didn't beat you?', the 'they' circled in pencil, Schneider offers additional subtext, 'Tramps caught by authorities' (Beckett, 1954, 7), in place, perhaps, of Pozzo's reference to potential 'highwaymen' (54). To Vladimir's 'muses on the struggle' to remove boots, or in this case shoes, Schneider adds another irritant, 'and wet pants' to account for Vladimir's 'legs wide apart, stiff strides' (7). And Schneider begins to incorporate Wilder's dialogue revisions soon after. Beckett's 'Get up till I embrace you' is rendered either as a replacement or as an explanation to the actors in his revised promptbook entry, 'Stand up so I can shake your hand' (Schneider, 1955, 1–1). Beckett's 'Ah stop blathering and help me off with this bloody thing' becomes in Schneider's promptbook, 'Ah stop shooting your mouth off and help me with this damn shoe' (p. L*2 [i.e., 1–2]). To Vladimir's reference to the pair's Eiffel Tower suicide fantasy, Schneider inserts Wilder's alternative wording: 'That time when everybody was jumping off the top of the Eiffel Tower, we should have done it then, among the first' (1–2). In the redrafted Grove Press copy that Wilder reworked, the alternative posed was, 'Hand in hand we should have thrown ourselves off the top of the Eiffel Tower, among the first to do it. We had decent clothes then' (Beckett, 1954, 7b). In either case, the alternatives tend to suggest deficiencies in Beckett's phrasing.

How many of such alternatives that Schneider was recording in his Wilderised Grove Press text and subsequently recasting into his promptbook were finally adopted in production is not always clear. Many of the comments were rephrased backstory or translations into an American idiom and the like for the actors. What is clear is that Schneider felt little authorial allegiance, even as such fealty was the position that he would subsequently adopt and espouse as his directorial trademark, what Natka Bianchini calls his 'directorial calling card'. Instead, in 1955, he felt quite at liberty to alter, to tinker, to retranslate, to rewrite the play of a neophyte, European playwright not conversant with the American idiom. Following Wilder's lead, Schneider redrafts the protagonists' comparative discourse on pain thus, for example: Estragon's 'It hurts?' becomes 'Does it hurt?' Vladimir's response becomes, 'Hurt! He wants to know does it hurt. Sure it hurts'. For Estragon's rejoinder,

Beckett's '(pointing)' is amplified to '(pointing with forefinger)' (pencilled thus in the Grove text, Beckett, 1954, 7b), then, 'You might button it all the same', is rewritten first to, 'You may as well button up just the same', and then more explicitly to, 'That's no reason for not buttoning up your pants' (Schneider, 1955, 1–4) ['That's no excuse for not buttoning up your pants' (Beckett, 1954, 7b)]. Too often, Wilder and Schneider render Beckett's profundities into trivialised responses: Beckett's 'Sometimes I feel it coming all the same. Then I go all queer', becomes at first, 'Sometimes I feel something coming just the same. Then I feel all funny', then, more fatalistically, if not simplistically, 'Sometimes I say to myself what's coming will come' (Schneider, 1955, 1–4). Beckett's 'How shall I say? Relieved and at the same time … (*He searches for the word*) … appalled. (*With emphasis*) AP-Palled' becomes, 'How do I explain it? It's a relief and at the same time it scares you. Really scares you' (1–4). In a revised typescript sent to Alan Simpson for the Dublin premiere, Beckett revised his translation from 'terror struck' to 'appalled' (TS p. 3, MS-TCD-10730; Beckett Digital Manuscript Project, hereafter BDMP, the Trinity College typescript designated ETP in the textual chronology). Of this typescript, the BDMP says 'Used and marked in rehearsals', but clearly the careful revisions to the typescript now at Trinity College are pre-rehearsal revisions and in Beckett's hand; rehearsal copies were retyped by the company.[8]

Beckett's branding of Pozzo's pipe as a 'Kapp and Peterson' becomes a 'Kaywoodie' in Miami (Schneider, 1955, 1–47), Wilder for a time entertaining an 'old corncob' in pencil, a 'Dunhill' in ink, and later a 'Meerschaum', again in pencil; Beckett's 'ten Francs' is transposed to 'a dime (quarter)' by Wilder who also suggested, 'I wouldn't mind a gold piece', followed by a reduction in the request to 'a silver piece' (Beckett, 1954, 26); 'a queer thing' becomes 'a strange thing' (2–3) with Wilder. Some of these alterations might be deemed 'improvements', as 'Show' becomes 'Let me see' (Schneider, 1955, 1–43), and 'There you are again', becomes, 'Here you are again'. Beckett's 'Would that be

---

[8] Corrections on the Pike Theatre TS p. 33 are particularly telling as Beckett changes the speaker for the response to Pozzo's 'You find it tedious' from Vladimir to Estragon for his 'Somewhat', and then has Vladimir respond 'I've been better entertained' as they appear in the Grove Press edition (Beckett, 1954, 26), revised from the original, Estragon's 'I've enjoyed myself more'. On TS p. 50, Beckett revised 'Find shelter' to the more idiomatic 'Take cover' (Beckett, 1954, 35), 'getting' is cut from 'It's getting cold', and on p. 51 Vladimir's affirmative repetition of Estragon, 'Yes, it's too late now', becomes 'No, it's not worthwhile now'. In this copy, however, the crucial opening to Lucky's speech is missing, TS p. 38. This is especially significant since Lucky's speech is the most heavily revised and marked up segment of this TS. The Boy's second appearance is also missing, pp. 92–5. Collation of the Pike TS with the Grove Press 1954 text is available at Dukes (1995a, *passim*). Transcription of this Pike Theatre TS is available at the BDMP as MS-TCD-10730 (ETP): www.beckettarchive-org.proxy.lib.fsu.edu/godot/MS-TCD-10730/p1?view=text

a help?' becomes, 'Would that help you?'; but 'stool' becomes 'folding chair' for some reason (Beckett, 1954, 24), and 'The Macon country' becomes the more celestial, 'The Garden of Eden' in Wilder's rendering (39b). Page 23b contains the ominous, 'Cut here and there'. Such alterations are pervasive in Wilder's retranslation and in Schneider's promptbook, and they deviate significantly from the Beckett-revised American text already in print, but Schneider's alterations follow the spirit and often the letter of Wilder's retranslation and his thematic existentialist preoccupations.

Wilderising Beckett

Wilder's involvement in *Godot*'s American staging began far earlier and was considerably more extensive than either Rosset or Beckett could have imagined. He had seen productions of *Godot* in Paris and again in London and had strong views about it. He had in fact been commissioned in 1953 to revise, adapt, revamp, retranslate, or 'doctor', in the terminology of Broadway, Beckett's French text. The need for a redo was reinforced when he read the author's translation in the newly revised Grove Press text, an earlier version of which he saw staged in London. Beckett would warn his French publisher against what he thought of as textual meddling, which he called 'this adaptation business', as requests for English-language rights for *En attendant Godot* began to arrive in Paris in mid-1953 (Beckett, 2011, 379). As Van Hulle and Verhulst write,

> The first serious offer came in May of that year, by the American writer-director Garson Kanin, with the financial backing of Harold L. Oram, a fundraiser for humanitarian and environmental causes. Because only a French version of *Godot* was available at the time, Kanin asked fellow American writer Thornton Wilder to translate and 'adapt' the text into English. (Van Hulle and Verhulst, 2018, 267; Beckett, 2011, 380n1)

Despite his warning, Beckett seems to have had only the scantest idea of how completely commercial theatre was imbricated in 'this adaptation business'. As early as May 1953, then, Beckett was responding to a specific proposition from the American writer and director, Kanin, a major figure in the American theatre who would be elected to the American Theater Hall of Fame in 1985. After Beckett's warning, his French publisher, Jérôme Lindon, working through the French producer Denise Tual, acknowledged that English-language performance rights were still available (Beckett, 2011, 380n1). Two days after he received the 'before' 18 May 1953 letter, Beckett received another enquiry, this from the London agent Rosica Colin, asking about the English-language rights to all of his work and, further, proposing a club performance of *Godot* to work around the anticipated objections of the Lord Chamberlain's office to some of the language in the play. Beckett replied to Colin on 19 May,

> Re English and American rights to my work in French I think you would be well advised to get in touch with my editor [i.e., publisher] Monsieur Jérôme Lindon [. . .]. He knows better than I how things stand. I am not even sure that they are still available. (Beckett, 2011, 380, 381n1)

While producers, theatre directors, actors, and translators have been theatre's chief 'adapters', Van Hulle and Verhulst point out that the BBC, too, was dissatisfied even with this Franco-Irishman's English:

> When the BBC received a copy of Beckett's early translation in late 1953, they found it 'basically phony', 'far less funny, and less racy, than in the original', requiring 'nothing less than a free hand' and thus permission to 'tinker' with the text[9] – which settled that matter for Beckett. (Van Hulle and Verhulst, 2018, 274)

Such resistance to Beckett's work remained at the BBC into November of 1955 after the success of *Godot* at the Criterion when at a meeting of radio drama staff on the issue of experimental productions, Val Gielgud, the noted actor John Gielgud's brother, proclaimed:

> 'Heaven defend us from an outbreak of *Godot*-scripts where the tricks only just hide an almost complete lack of anything to say'. The day was saved by then script editor Barbara Bray who replied, 'Third Programme planners will have to be prepared not only to be daring initially but also to persist in the face of possible audience resistance long enough for public taste to accommodate itself. (Gielgud and Bray qtd in Kynaston, 2010, 517)

Soon after, the *Evening Standard* drama awards were held (for the first time),[10] and despite resistance to awarding *Waiting for Godot* 'best play', a compromise was reached. *Godot* would receive the prize for 'most controversial' play of the year (Kynaston, 2010, 517), a dubious distinction, at best. Soon after the award, however, the BBC would commission a radio play from Beckett, and he responded with *All That Fall*, which Faber & Faber would quickly announce as

---

9 The Bowdlerised initial Faber & Faber publication of *Godot* would not be the only instance of British institutions censoring Beckett's texts for performance. The BBC, too, would feel free to 'tinker', to quietly alter a Beckett play, as they did with the 24 June 1959 radio broadcast of *Embers* (see Gontarski, 1999, 127–32).

10 No stranger to controversy in drama, the *Evening Standard* would award Tennessee Williams' still controversial *Sweet Bird of Youth* the 'best play' award for 1958. It, too, was directed by Peter Hall at the New Watergate Theatre Club at the Comedy Theatre, and, as a 'Theatre Club' production, it too lay outside the reach of the Lord Chamberlain's office. Hall would initially direct Williams' much less controversial *Camino Real* in 1957, and this interest in Williams immediately after *Waiting for Godot* may explain why Hall was unavailable for *Godot*'s UK tour or its American premiere.

'Also by Samuel Beckett' on the page facing the title page and on the dust wrapper to its first edition of *Waiting for Godot*.

The strictures he would subsequently impose on performances of his theatre works were one response to Beckett's reservations about adaptation as he was being drawn into the commercial theatre world where adaptation was the norm, although he would be less than consistent, even whimsical at times in enforcing those strictures. In 1953, however, Beckett's response to the possibility of 'adaptation' now seems understated. He appears to have intuited, at least, that his theatre work had something of a flexibility, an elasticity – in short, an adaptability – to the point, at times, of multiple configurations. The author himself would finally enter 'this adaptation business' to recast his work through his various and multiple creative roles, and he understood, finally – if slowly, perhaps – that theatre by its nature is malleable, that is, all performance is adaptation. He subsequently met extensively with the designated American director Alan Schneider who crossed the Atlantic with fellow passenger Thornton Wilder, the latter sailing to Rome, the former through Cannes to Paris to meet with Beckett and thence to London to see Peter Hall's staging of *Godot*. Schneider had been at best Myerberg's third directorial choice. In a *New York Times* excerpt from his autobiography, Schneider notes that, 'For "Godot" he [Myerberg] had wanted Garson Kanin, but Gar suddenly became either unavailable or uncertain about the project's prospects' (Schneider, 1985, 47). In fact, Myerberg's first choice, following Albery's lead, had been Peter Hall, who, too, became unavailable, even for the play's subsequent London and UK tour, as Beckett informed Rosset:

> So far as I know still no complaints from Piccadilly [location of the Criterion Theatre] and Albery, when I saw him here was it last week, was optimistic about further prospects. He told me that Peter Hall, who directed in London, had been invited to direct New York production but might not be able to get away. No news since. (Beckett, 2011, 570)

On 25 October 1955, the New York situation still in flux, Rosset could finally offer some encouraging news to Beckett barely a month before Miami rehearsals were scheduled to begin and that included an invitation to participate (to one degree or another) in the American production:

> Just spoke to the would be producer of *Godot*, Michael Myerberg, who says he would like you to come here and to that end he will pay all expenses of the trip. Of course to me this sounds wonderful. He adds that Garson Kanin might be the director and that Kanin wants you to be here to advise him. SO ! ! What is your reaction? I certainly hope you accept. (see SULSC, Box 104)

The offer, if accepted, might have recast the American premiere by allowing Beckett more involvement in the production than was the case in London, but he declined, well, almost, on 12 November 1955 in his inimitable if evasive way while observing etiquette protocols in the process:

> Thanks for your letters and Myerburg [*sic*] news. I am very touched by his offer to pay my expenses if I go to New York. As he has not written to me personally I leave to you the conveyance of my very warm thanks. I do not want to say definitely yes or no just now, gored insufficiently by the old horns [of a dilemma, say]. I suppose it will alas be no as usual. If it were just to give the director of production a hand, without getting in his way, or letting him get in mine, and then exemption from interviews, journalists, fool answers to fool questions and kindred miseries, then I would consider going very seriously. But it is obvious I cannot accept such a generous offer and then not do what is expected of me. If there is one thing I cannot do it is talk about my work, or 'explain' it, except perhaps over the third bottle with an indulgent friend. (Beckett, 2011, 567)

Beckett's decision was thus deferred, at least until he met the American director after which he would make his decision on an American crossing. He would subsequently say on 20 November 1955:

> I look forward to meeting Schneider next Saturday. I saw his *Skin* [*of Our Teeth*] here at the last festival. I did not much like it. If I feel he is amenable to my distant ccrebrations and that there is really a chance of my helping him, and the play, then I'm your man, now that I know myself absolved by Myerberg from performing apery. (Beckett, 2011, 568)

In the same letter, Beckett would also note, 'I have seen photos of the Criterion set-up, all wrong I think. I suppose Scheider [*sic*] will pause in London to see the production. I feel rather glad now that Hall is not available for USA' (Beckett, 2011, 568).

By mid-November 1955, then, Schneider was the newly appointed director of *Godot*, a decision, it turns out, made on Wilder's advice to Myerberg who had produced the original 1942 Broadway production of Wilder's *The Skin of Our Teeth*, directed by Elia Kazan with Tallulah Bankhead and Frederic March, and which would win the Pulitzer Prize for drama in 1943. Its title derives from the 'Book of Job', 19:20, 'My bone cleaveth to my skin and to my flesh, and I am escaped with the skin of my teeth', and the convention-breaking, myth-driven play is laden with overt biblical imagery with a focus on the genesis of humanity. Some critics, particularly Joseph Campbell and Henry Morton Robinson, have detected other sources and have seen Wilder's play as, if not derived from, at least heavily indebted to or even an appropriation of James Joyce's *Finnegans Wake*. That is, the suggestion was that by 1942 Wilder was already rewriting or adapting not only biblical but contemporary avant-garde material for the Broadway stage. Campbell and Robinson went public with their findings, publishing 'The Skin of *Whose* Teeth?' in the *Saturday Review* barely a month after the play's Broadway opening, and further they wrote to the Pulitzer Prize committee directly to make it aware of their findings – to no effect, however. Their conclusions were drawn from their work on the pioneering and very influential study *A Skeleton Key to Finnegans Wake*, published in 1944, only five years after Joyce's final novel appeared. Work on their *Skeleton Key* led them to conclude that 'Mr. Wilder's play, *The Skin of our Teeth*, was not entirely an original composition but an Americanized recreation, thinly disguised, of James Joyce's *Finnegans Wake*' (Campbell, 2003, 257), and that such a level of borrowing in Wilder's play, they concluded, went far beyond the bounds of what was professionally and ethically acceptable: 'Important plot elements', they continue, 'characters, devices of presentation, as well as major themes and many of the speeches, are directly and frankly imitated, but with the flimsy veneer to lend an American touch to the original features' (257). As they recount parallels, they note, 'There are, in fact, no end of the meticulous unacknowledged copyings' (259).

Schneider revived Wilder's atavistic comedy, with Helen Hayes and Mary Martin for star power. It opened at the Théâtre Sarah Bernhardt in Paris in 1955, one of the American productions to take part in a 'Salute to Paris' tribute. Beckett saw it but was less than impressed by it. Myerberg and Wilder, then, had the credentials, reputation, and theatrical savvy to bring Beckett's experimental 'tragicomedy' to the Broadway stage, and Schneider was becoming part of their team, their up-and-coming director, but the danger that neither Beckett nor Rosset, at this point, could foresee was the looming shadow of Thornton Wilder. He would reshape *Waiting for Godot* to become something of a sequel to *The Skin of Our Teeth*, producing, thus, a pair of atavistic 'tragicomedies'.

The original plan was to have *Waiting for Godot* open at the Coconut Grove Playhouse near Miami Beach, Florida on 3 January 1956, which it did, then play Washington DC, Boston, and Philadelphia before opening at the Music Box Theater on Broadway on 16 February, which it did not. The play closed in Miami Beach on 14 January, and the director was summarily discharged, although subsequently Schneider would suggest that he was otherwise engaged for subsequent productions of the play: 'He was unavailable for Myerberg's *second try* at the play', this presumably the New York premiere (Levy, 1956, 35; emphasis added). This 'second try' terminology was a deliberate stratagem, a means for the producer to distance himself from the Miami production and, more important, legally from its director, but Myerberg was also under pressure from competing producers. Beckett wrote to Rosset on 11 February 1955: 'A letter from Leo Kerz of the New Repertory Theatre asking for permission to put on for 8 weeks on Broadway with

Buster Keaton, Brando, Wally Cox and/or Fred Allen'. But, as Beckett admitted, 'It was bitter to have to refuse, as I had to [since] the star-haunted Glenville has withdrawn and Albery acquired for himself exclusively a further 6 months option on UK and USA rights' (see SULSC, Box 104). Albery's extension kept Myerberg in play in the United States. Four days later, 15 February 1955, Rosset wrote:

> One success after another rolling up in Europe – and nothing on Broadway. Poor Mr. Albery is going to have the greatest mountain of blame ever piled up if something is not forthcoming within a reasonable time here in New York. (Rosset, 2017, 85)

Rosset returns to the issue of delay on 30 March:

> Sorry to hear that news from London is scant and unpromising because there have been several opportunities here to put on the play. It still seems a shame not to have some kind of performance in New York, and the time is not yet too late if London should finally be abandoned by you. (see SULSC, Box 104)

That is, if the play did not, finally, open at the Arts in August 1955.

Myerberg had closed the play in Miami as part of a legal stratagem that allowed him to remove Schneider as director and so, technically, to be released from all contractual obligations with the director. The scheduled 16 February opening at the Music Box Theater in New York was thus forfeited, and the play's cast was disbanded. The April rescheduling for New York would thus be a second production, a revival, say, deemed a new production, separate from and not a continuation of the Miami try-out, hence the change of cast (except for Lahr, the principal draw) and, finally, and perhaps most significantly, of both director and text. Myerberg's public phrasing is thus pertinent here. After the Miami closing, he would tell journalists, 'When I do it again … ', 'the next time', and 'I intend to do it again as soon as I can', thereby punctuating the fact that the Miami venture was over, closed, finished, the terms of those contracts no longer in effect (Levy, 1956, 35). This became an important distinction, although Van Hulle and Verhulst refer to the Broadway production as a 'transfer' (Van Hulle and Verhulst, 2018, 164). In Myerberg's strategy, New York was a separately created production, neither a continuation nor a transfer. He would also reverse his approach to publicity for what he now deemed a revival, and he would caution New York audiences with a notice in the *New York Times*: 'I respectfully suggest that those who come to the theater for casual entertainment do not buy a ticket to this attraction' (Levy, 1956, 96).

Schneider had been set (or set up) from the first to become part of what was Myerberg's Wilderisation plan, and the text that Schneider was working with in Miami was a retyping (on something like onion-skin paper since handwritten

notes on the following page are visible through the typed page) of the hardcover
Grove Press edition, the retyping perhaps commissioned by Donald Albery
since the handwritten note at the bottom of the typed title page bears Albery's
London address. In his autobiography, *Entrances*, the director makes little
mention of the text he was using (and freely altering, as it turns out), with
rehearsals beginning 9 December 1955:

> Myerberg insisted that I go to Paris to consult with the author and to London
> to see Peter Hall's production of *Godot*, which had recently opened at the Arts
> Theater. After repeated requests, or rather demands, from Myerberg to
> Beckett's agent in London, the playwright had reluctantly agreed to meet
> with 'the New York director' – I don't think Beckett knew my name – for half
> an hour. [. . .] Wilder had evidently informed Myerberg that he could clear up
> whatever difficulties I might have had in interpreting the script of *Godot*; in
> fact, he might be able to *improve* on Mr. Beckett's own translation of his
> original French text into English, which Mr. Wilder did not particularly
> admire, although he considered *Godot* one of the two greatest modern
> plays. (Schneider, 1985, 47; emphasis added)

Wilder, in fact, wrote to Kay Boyle on 29 August 1958 of his admiration for
Beckett: 'Yes, Indeed, I would wish to join all those who express appreciation
for Samuel Beckett (I saw *Godot* twice in Paris; once in London; once in
New York). And I read and re-read the other plays and novels, and eagerly
wait for more' (Wilder and Bryer, 2008, 556).

Schneider says that 'Myerberg insisted I go to Paris', but his formal contract,
as article 11, section b stipulates, is for a trip to London:

> I [Myerberg] further agree to provide you with round trip first class transpor-
> tation from New York to London in order for you to observe the London
> production of the play. I shall reimburse you for all out of pocket expenses
> incurred by you during your travel and stay in London for the aforementioned
> purpose. (UCSD Alan Schneider Papers, MSS 0103, Box 10, Folder 19)

The Paris expenses and the length of Schneider's stay abroad subsequently
would become points of contention. On that 'first class' Atlantic crossing,
Schneider notes of his meetings with Wilder:

> We met regularly to go over the lines. [. . .] He started with suggestions for
> changing a few of them. By the time we got to Cannes, he had changed almost
> every single one, including the whole of Lucky's speech. (Schneider, 1986, 223)

In something of an understatement, Schneider goes on to say that 'So detailed and
regular were our daily meetings that a rumor later circulated that Wilder had
rewritten the play. Thornton may have been amused by that thought; Beckett was
not' (Schneider, 1986, 223). While the Wilder revisions are indeed extensive, none

of the documents, neither the Wilder revisions of the Grove Press text nor Schneider's separately retyped promptbook, supports the director's claim that Wilder had rewritten 'the whole of Lucky's speech'. In Wilder's rendering, Lucky's speech, it turns out, is among the least tampered with portion of the entire play. Lucky was allowed his quirky language by Wilder, Didi and Gogo were not. Beckett's alterations from his first preliminary typescript to the revisions for Grove Press, on the other hand, show considerable rewriting of Lucky's speech.

It seems at least curious if not evasive that Schneider would refer to Wilder's retranslation of the play as a 'rumor', since he also admits that Wilder 'had changed almost every single one [line]', and Schneider finally worked with and through Wilder's thoroughly reworked copy of the play for his initial staging. The hardback Grove Press edition, the revisions to which Wilder dictated in his rewriting, contains Schneider's personal details, his and Beckett's home addresses, Albery's business address, and it is branded with Wilder's initials, 'TW', under which is noted, 'Working Copy / Nov.-Dec. 1955', all jotted on the book's endpapers. The 'TW' initials appear regularly in the text (see Figure 2, for instance) to suggest that Schneider was functioning like an assistant to or a scribe for Wilder. Schneider's copy directly affirms, 'Thornton Wilder's re-translation of Godot for AS, Nov-Dec, 1955', the physical copy of which is now on deposit in the Schneider archive at the University of California – San Diego (UCSD).[11] In fact, the Schneider/Wilder copy suggests that their meetings began in New York before their Atlantic crossing and carried over into Cannes after it. Schneider's understanding of, and so his staging of the play in Miami was thus not only deeply informed by Wilder's retranslation, but Beckett's work became significantly Wilderised.

When Myerberg spoke about the production after its Miami failure, however, he tended to sound like its director:

> I went too far in my efforts to give the play a base for popular acceptance. I accented the wrong things in trying to illuminate corners of the text that remained in the shadows in the London production. For instance, I cast the play too close to type. In casting Bert Lahr and Tom Ewell I created the wrong impression about the play. (Levy, 1956, 33, 35; qtd in Knowlson, 1996, 378)

Although Alan Levy announces at the opening of his essay that the New York production of the play would finally open 'On April 19 – with new cast, new staging but the identical script', he is contradicted by Myerberg in the same essay. Myerberg admits to having made changes to the Miami text, but for New York he would return to the text as written: 'when I do it again I'm not

---

[11] UCSD Alan Schneider Papers, box 74, folder 14. Special Collections describes the item as follows, 'WAITING FOR GODOT. Grove Press, New York. Title page inscribed Thornton Wilder's re-translation of *Godot* for Alan Schneider, 1955'.

going to change the script. Every revision we tried proved to be false' (Levy, 1956, 33, 35).[12] Myerberg's admission represents a stunning reversal of strategy as he essentially changes allegiances, from Wilder to Beckett. In keeping with that reversal, he fired his Wilderising Miami director and returned to the text of the play that Beckett wrote.

Surprisingly few critics have dug into the details of the Miami *Godot* production even as the available archival and published material is copious. One who did is Natka Bianchini in her monograph *The Legacy of Alan Schneider as Beckett's American Director*, especially in her opening chapter, 'The Laugh *Sensation* of Two Continents!' or as Schneider remembers, 'Bert Lahr, star of "Harvey," and Tom Ewell, star of "The Seven Year Itch," in the Laugh Sensation of Two Continents, "Waiting for Godot"' (Schneider, 1971, 1). Her approach is to redress a perceived 'omission in Beckett scholarship' (Bianchini, 2015, xiii) because the Beckett and Schneider 'artistic collaboration has never been critically studied as a partnership that has profoundly influenced American theater in the mid- to late twentieth century' (1). Any number of critics have applauded that achievement, which, on the whole, Bianchini accomplishes deftly. Our purposes here are more narrowly conceived, however, focusing on Schneider's initial approach to a theatrical text that baffled him. Bianchini does a thorough job detailing the Schneider–Myerberg correspondence held at the University of California – San Diego, and she provides a full account of the last-minute decision to open the play near Miami, Florida, in Coral Gables, and not, as originally planned, in Washington DC, an economically driven decision based on monetary incentives generated by the two stars involved in the production, Lahr and Ewell, or as Schneider put it, 'at a handsome guarantee-against-loss for the producer' (Schneider, 1971, 1). Myerberg's desire to please his star actors, she notes, 'meant running roughshod over Beckett's text' (Bianchini, 2015, 26). And she applauds Schneider's struggles to keep the set as unlocalised and unspecified as possible: 'Schneider discovered that Myerberg had also interfered with the production's scenic design' (24). But she too easily accepts and repeats what has become the received wisdom of Schneider's directorial ethos: 'As a director, Schneider's calling card was fidelity to the text of the author' (5). That would eventually become the case, but it was not so in 1955–6. For one, Bianchini, stops short of examining the full *textual* evidence available in the Schneider archive so she can accept Schneider's version of Wilder's

---

[12] Levy also cites the date of the Paris production as 'one winter evening in 1952' (Levy, 1956, 33); it was 3 January 1953, actually. See 'Production Photographs of *Waiting for Godot* by Samuel Beckett (1953 Premiere at the Théâtre de Babylone, Paris)', British Library: www.bl.uk/collection-items/photographs-of-waiting-for-godot-by-samuel-beckett-1953

relationship to the Miami production, the one recounted in Schneider's autobiography: 'The two spent so much time together that after the [transatlantic]
trip *a rumor emerged, completely erroneous*, that Wilder had "rewritten"
Beckett's script', somehow missing Schneider's admission that Wilder 'had
changed almost every single one [line]' (Bianchini, 2015, 158n39; emphasis
added). At best, she admits that 'It was likely he was influenced by Thornton
Wilder, his traveling companion on the ocean liner from New York to France
before his first meeting with Beckett' (28). The implication is that, after
Schneider's meetings with Beckett, the director would follow the author's
lead. As we contend here, however, the archived texts and Wilder's selected
letters tell quite a different story. She also details Schneider's existentialist
preoccupations (27–8), which Beckett finally rejected out of hand at their
Paris and London meetings, but she stops short of attributing such views
directly to Wilder (see especially Schneider's note, 'TW [. . .] 4. Explain
Existentialism: lecture',[13] and his comment, 'Avoidance of night', which for
Schneider meant death, is followed below by 'Comments on being and doing'
with an arrow leading directly to 'Act of will with the day=Exist [existential-
ist] thing', the latter comment attributed directly to 'TW'; Beckett, 1954, 41).

Schneider is fully in the existentialist camp here despite Beckett's dismissal
of any connection. Bianchini draws her principal conclusions from Schneider's
'director's notebook': 'a small spiral bound steno pad filled with handwritten
notes' (Bianchini, 2015, 25, 27), at least some of which he forwarded to Beckett
(29–30), but with no mention of the full Wilder translation. She cites
Schneider's 'promptbooks' (25), at least in name, but does not mention what
amounts to the director's textual assault therein. Those notes on changes that
Schneider sent to Beckett, at least those he was willing to admit to, appear fully
neither in Harmon's edition of the Beckett–Schneider correspondence (1998)
nor in the *Letters of Samuel Beckett* (2011), but Beckett did respond to them on
27 December 1955, a week before the Miami opening. He queried the set, for
one, which tended to follow the London model: 'Why the platform? Is it just
rising ground?'; and he acknowledges gracefully other changes Schneider
made: 'Good of you to send me a list of your changes. If I had not met you
I'd be on a hot griddle!' (Beckett and Schneider, 1998, 6–7; Beckett, 2011, 586–
7). Beckett raises the issue of Wilder's rumoured intervention, as well, but
Schneider makes no mention directly of Wilder, as Bianchini never references
the fully Wilderised text; that is, she, like Schneider, avoids all mention of the

---

[13] Point 5 is left blank, but beneath it is a reference to page 41 of the Grove text, the point in the play
where V. and E. discuss 'thinking'.

completely redrafted version of the play that Wilder dictated to the director during their Atlantic crossing.

The endpapers to Schneider's copy of the Wilderised *Godot* testify to Wilder's co-option not only of Beckett's play but of the director himself. The revised script is filled with scribblings that might be considered the wisdom of Wilder. Schneider notes, for example, 'Theatre vs. novel (past)→specific – why we experience universal – shared – myth'. This is very much a restatement of Wilder that will appear shortly thereafter in Wilder's 'Preface' to *Three Plays* thus: 'The novel is pre-eminently the vehicle of the unique occasion [that is, 'specific'], the theater of the generalized one' (Wilder, 1957, xi), which for Wilder meant theatre's engagement with myth (that is, 'shared – myth').

Schneider also thinks through the relationship between theatre and thinking, 'Parody of avoiding thought in modern man?', then references 'TW', 'Whole history of human civilization / If no thinking people would have killed selves' (Beckett, 1954, 41b). The top of page 41b includes Schneider's comments on Wilder's explanation about this now heavily rewritten dialogue sequence about the thinking process as he notes in a box labelled 'TW': 'a, b, c, d, e & f'; that is, this is a logical sequence of thought about the process of avoiding thinking. The proposed dialogue to accompany Wilder's 'lecture' is, as Schneider notes, 'And that will prevent our getting back to that damned thinking', with, apparently, Estragon's response that leads to another conversational dead end, 'And after that, Didi?' (Beckett, 1954, 41b). Such evasion of thinking restates Wilder's entire assessment of the rise of the middle class from the mid-nineteenth century and its effect on theatre. Even as the middle class 'thronged to Shakespeare', Wilder asks, 'How did they shield themselves against his probing? How did they smother the theater [. . .]?' (Wilder, 1957, x). When Schneider speaks in what appears to be his own voice, infrequent as that is, he ruminates mostly on stagecraft, attributing such comments directly to himself with an autograph 'AS': 'nineteenth century realism [. . .] with real food, decorative, plush furniture, etc.', rejecting 'picture frame' theatre, which 'says, let's look at a pretty picture' in favour of '[gradual loss – to essentials – AS]'. But the 'AS' is clearly an internalisation of 'TW' and Wilder's assault on the rise of the middle class in the nineteenth century as, 'the middle class devitalized the theater' – it 'loaded the stage with specific objects, because every concrete object on stage fixes and narrows the action to one moment in time and space'. These are particularisations that obscure the universal and mythic, the true concerns of theatre, according to Wilder. He punctuates his point by noting the lack of such particularisation in Shakespeare and classic Spanish drama: 'There are not even chairs on the English or Spanish stages in the time of Elizabeth I' (Wilder, 1957, xi). The emphasis on particulars is for Wilder 'childish attempts to be "real"' (xi). Schneider echoes this with, 'Open stage' that 'enables} our mind to follow without eye distraction' / 'freeer}'. This, too, is straight from what will appear in Wilder's 'Preface' to *Three Plays* the following year, as he decries the middle-class preferences for 'The box set [...] the curtain, the proscenium', which 'boxed the action', and 'they [the middle class] increasingly shut the play up into a museum showcase' (x).

As with much archival research, handwriting is often an issue, and illegibility often inhibits and complicates readings and transcriptions, especially those annotations made hurriedly in pencil, as many notes are in Schneider's redrafted text and promptbook, but not all of Schneider's annotations are unreadable. Bianchini, however, seems unaware of what Schneider freely labels 'Wilder's re-translation' (Figure 1) – and Schneider himself avoids addressing the retranslation to Beckett and forthrightly in his autobiography.[14] The Wilder document is freely referenced in printed records, however. Penelope Niven's (2012) biography of Wilder surprisingly makes no mention of Beckett or Schneider, but Gilbert A. Harrison's earlier biography, *The Enthusiast* (1983), lays out the entire Wilder and Schneider relationship in a single sentence, although his dating of the encounter differs slightly from Schneider's: Wilder in October 1955 'was back in Europe, having idled his days aboard the *SS United States* dictating a translation of Samuel Beckett's *Waiting for Godot* to Alan Schneider' (Harrison, 1983, 326). That sentence is confirmed in a letter Wilder sent to Thew Wright, Jr. on 28 November 1955 complaining about his boredom on the Atlantic crossing, adding:

> Myerberg put Alan Schneider on the boat to pick my brain about their forthcoming production of *Waiting for Godot* (Bert Lahr, Tom Ewell!) and sure – free gratis for nothing I retranslated by dictation the whole play ... rather enjoyed it but it took time and mind and energy from other things. (Wilder and Bryer, 2008, 537–8)

When the *New York Times* theatre critic Mel Gussow reviewed a 1988 revival of Wilder's *Our Town*, he returned to this encounter of Wilder and Schneider with early Beckett but with decidedly more emphasis on Wilder's influence on Schneider's thinking than Schneider admits:

> Wilder [...] felt he knew exactly what the play [*Waiting for Godot*] was about and proceeded to give Mr. Schneider a line-by-line analysis. At Wilder's

---

[14] Van Hulle and Verhulst, in turn, do acknowledge and refer to Wilder's retranslation: '*In his re-translation* of *Waiting for Godot* Thornton Wilder also seized on this passage to avoid confusion between the English and Americans: "Those British say cawm (*Pause.*) What they are is a calm people"' (UCSD, Alan Schneider papers, box 74, folder 14). It is clear that Wilder is using the second impression of *En attendant Godot* where Beckett added the line: "Ce sont des gens câââms" (1953, 24; 1970a, 20; 1971a, 20)' (Van Hulle and Verhulst, 2018, 304; emphasis added).

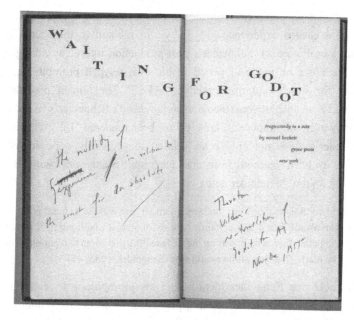

Figure 1 Alan Schneider's published copy of the American edition of *Waiting
for Godot* with Thornton Wilder's dictated translation of the play.

> recommendation, Mr. Schneider had just been hired to direct the first American
> production of 'Godot', and he listened intently, as Wilder told him that the play
> was an existential work about 'the nullity of experience in relation to the search
> for an absolute.' The director eventually realized that Wilder, acting as irrepress-
> ible scholar, *was in effect rewriting 'Godot' and re-envisioning it as if it were
> a work of his own.* (Gussow, 1988, 7; emphasis added)

What Gussow did not fully apprehend, nor Schneider openly acknowledge, is
how completely Wilder's emphasis on 'the nullity of experience' shaped the
director's conception of the play. Characterising the production soon after its
Miami closing, Schneider echoed Wilder's analysis (via Camus, perhaps): 'Godot
means certainty. Night means death. It shows the nullity of life and it means
nothing. In the awareness that there is no meaning to life, there is meaning' (Levy,
1956, 35; Bianchini, 2015, 27–8). The comment Schneider scribbles onto the title
page of the 1954, hardback, Grove Press, Wilderised copy of *Godot*, having taken

Wilder's dictation, complete with the scribe's correction, is as follows: 'The nullity of ~~existence~~ experience _____/_____ in relation to the search for an absolute' (see Figure 1). Schneider's post-production interview talking points reprise the notes he made in pencil in his own retyped promptbook: 'Man searching for some kind of certainty – ALS'; 'The human predicament'; 'Reaching for an absolute impossible to comprehend'. Schneider's 'ALS' designation, however, might more accurately have been rendered 'TW'. That is, most of Schneider's notes not only echo Wilder; they directly opposed what he professed to have learned from his forthright discussions with Beckett. 'According to him', Schneider notes,

> Godot had 'no meaning' and 'no symbolism'. There was no 'general point of
> view involved', but it was certainly 'not existentialist'. Nothing in it meant
> anything other than what it was on the surface. 'It's just about two people who
> are like that'. That was all he would say. (Schneider, 1985, 47)

The one note that Schneider identifies in his promptbook as coming from Beckett is pencilled onto the opening page, amid a welter of Wilder quotes. Beckett would reprise the comment with any number of other directors, or at least he would offer variations on the metaphor to characterise the play: 'A sea of Time surrounds the boat of this play, / & leaks into it – S. B'. On the following page, Schneider begins trying to specify something of this 'sea of Time' with the rubric 'Take time': 'Est. [Estragon] seated / off C [centre] in relation / to tree'; 'Struggle how ~~on~~ going on'; 'to get / boot (shoe) / off'. And a page later he notes, 'They've been waiting always and forever'. In the opening sequence of the Wilder dictated retranslation of the play, however, Schneider notes and highlights Wilder's observation on time, which seems to run counter to Beckett's: 'Keep in continuous present' (Beckett, 1954, 7). The comment is enclosed in a drawn black box for emphasis and is marked with the initials 'TW'. The *absence* of 'A sea of Time', or at least the absence of leakage, in Wilder's view, may have helped Schneider account for the characters' having such difficulty with day-to-day memory. In response to Pozzo's preoccupation with his watch, Vladimir opines, 'Time has stopped' (Beckett, 1954, 24b), suggesting a continuous, changeless present, the felt experience of waiting, their waiting, as Schneider notes, 'always and forever'. But Schneider seems confused between Wilder's 'Keep in continuous present' and Beckett's leaking time. As Vladimir makes reference to the inauguration of the Eiffel Tower, 'in the nineties', that is, after its opening in March of 1889, Schneider reads the date reference as '1900's', as Beckett's 'a million years ago' becomes 'a long time back there in 1900', as he notes in the Wilderised text (Beckett, 1954, 7b).

Through Schneider, Wilder rewrote Beckett's script in any number of ways: 'We were dressed right in those days' (in pencil), or 'We had decent clothes in those days' (in pen, Beckett, 1954, 7b). Schneider's note finally is: '1900: [in pencil] That time when everybody [was] jumping off we should have done it then. [In pen] We should have been [?]' (Beckett, 1954, 7b). Even as Schneider professed guidance from Beckett and his stated attempts to work through time's seeping, leaking into the play, he apparently decided to remain on the Wilder, Myerberg, and, perhaps, the Vladimir team.

Schneider's version of these events, finally, what amounts to his rewriting of history, has been so successful that when Clive Barnes reviewed a series of one-acts that Schneider directed at the Arena Stage's Kreger Theater in Washington DC, in 1976, he could state overtly, and astonishingly, in a review dominated by cliches and filled with repeated errors, including the statement that Beckett was James Joyce's secretary and that his 'use of language in the stream-of-consciousness fashion is totally Joycean', that Schneider 'has justifiably established himself as Beckett's American mentor', reversing, perhaps, the roles of teacher and student, mentor and protégé. The nature of the mentor–protégé relationship is clearly laid out, however, in the Schneider–Beckett correspondence (Beckett and Schneider, 1998, *passim*). As Barnes struggles for profundity, he can at best echo Schneider's and thereby Wilder's preoccupation with death in Beckett's play, 'Night is death' in Schneider's phrase: 'What is Beckett trying to say to us? He is trying to say that we are going to die.' (Barnes, 1976, 64). How – well – existential. And Bianchini herself cannot quite abandon this thread, although, admittedly, she follows Schneider's lead here. Of his 1971 off-Broadway revival of *Godot* at the Sheridan Square Playhouse in New York, for which Grove Press published its now-famous booklet 'A Discussion Guide for the Play *Waiting for Godot*', part of a strategy the press adopted to generate academic interest for the play and its author, she notes that now in this fourth staging of the play, what amount to Schneider's Wilderean preoccupations persist as she finds:

> the same themes that he articulated 15 years earlier in his notes for the Miami production [. . .]. His central theme remained that of 'man searching for some kind of certainty.' On the front page of his promptbook for this [1971] production Schneider wrote underneath the play's title, 'A music-hall sketch for two clowns out of Kafka and Camus, written by an Irish humorist with a French mind, Samuel Beckett,' a note that underscores both the comedy and the existentialism at the core of the play. (Bianchini, 2015, 96)

That is, Schneider remains the Wilder protégé, working through Wilder's preoccupations and referencing his mentor's assigned reading list.

3 *Godot*'s Bad Blood: Firing the Director, Rescuing the Play

A substantial amount of bad *Godot* blood was shed during the two-week Miami try-out, and it continued for several years beyond the play's Miami closing. That is, the 1956 closing of *Waiting for Godot* in Miami, Florida and the cancellation of the other planned pre-Broadway venues led to an acrimonious exchange between producer and director as a legal battle ensued when Schneider filed suit in the case identified as *Schneider* vs. *Myerberg*. While such suits amount to legal and financial haggling between aggrieved parties, the scuffle in this case opened a number of larger issues involving the nature of American commercial theatre in which Beckett found himself mired. When Bianchini cites the conflict, her focus is almost exclusively on Myerberg's insufficient compensation for Schneider's work in Miami, for expenses and contractual royalties for the Florida performances (Bianchini, 2015, 36–7). The larger and more fundamental issues, however, involve the nature of commercial theatre contracts and compensation packages, particularly the royalties due Schneider that, in this case, would have accrued had he directed the New York production. This would become the legal basis for assessing the 'damages' Schneider is said to have sustained as a result of Myerberg's alleged contract violations. In the business of commercial theatre these are called 'continuing royalties', usually a weekly royalty for as long as the show runs. Such royalties are often considered 'the real pay for the director' since rehearsal pay is often minimal. The principal issues, then, were connected to but larger than compensation for the Florida production. In particular, the central issue was whether Myerberg had violated Schneider's contract when he fired him and subsequently created a new production (but using the same production company with the same investors) for New York with Herbert Berghof as the director, and with, except for Bert Lahr, a new cast, thus denying Schneider his contractual continuing royalty.

In his notes on the legal action, Schneider admits that Myerberg fired him for 'Failure to perform', noting in particular that, in the face of negative audience response, particularly boisterous early departures, the director had refused to continue rehearsing the play after its opening. Schneider's file on the lawsuit contains a letter from Arthur Malet, who was both assistant stage manager to the company and an actor who played Lucky in half of the Miami performances.[15] In his letter of support for the director in this arbitration, dated 7 March 1957, Malet notes,

> I particularly recall his desire to hold rehearsals after the production had opened, and the rather summary objections and rejection of this on the part of the producer. Certainly it is far from Mr. Schneider's fault that rehearsals were not held. (UCSD, Alan Schneider Papers, MSS 103, Box 10, Folder 19)

---

[15] These legal issues aired and reviewed in a public hearing are thus part of a public record. Document copies are held in the Alan Schneider Archive at UCSD, the documents in MSS 103, Box 10, Folder 19. These documents constitute public legal testimony.

Bert Lahr, too, would offer support in a letter also dated 7 March 1957:

> It's my understanding that Mr. Myerberg is claiming he asked Schneider to hold rehearsals after the Florida opening and that Mr. Schneider refused. That is not true. I have no recollection whatsoever on the subject of rehearsals during the first week the show played in Miami, but I remember very distinctly Mr. Schneider having asked me if I wanted to rehearse during the second week but I refused [autograph revision to 'did not think it was necessary'] due to the fact that the show was closing and I thought rehearsals would be useless. (UCSD, Alan Schneider Papers, MSS 103, Box 10, Folder 19)

The fact that Lahr wrote in support of Schneider at all is surprising given the assessment of that relationship by his son, the *New Yorker* theatre critic John Lahr: 'In Florida, he was at war with the audience, with Tom Ewell, who played Vladimir, and, most of all, with the director, Alan Schneider, whose name was forever banned from our dinner-table conversation' (Lahr, 2009). Rosset summarised Schneider's opinion of actor relations in Miami for Beckett as follows: 'Bert Lahr and Ewell played against each other. [. . .] He [Lahr] does not play for the play but for himself. [. . .] In Miami Lahr and Ewell played two different plays' (Rosset, 2017, 118). The politics of the Miami venture lingered well into the following decades. When Martin Gottfried savaged Schneider's 1972 production of *Krapp's Last Tape* at Lincoln Center, writing in *Women's Wear Daily* that the director 'mutilated this exquisite and touching farewell to love. Beckett's trust of Schneider was never more misplaced' (Gottfried qtd in Bianchini, 2015, 111–12), Schneider defended himself to Beckett by arguing that the criticism was a personal attack: 'He is married to Lahr's daughter and has been out to get me for years' (Beckett and Schneider, 1998, 295). Ewell, on the other hand, reunited with Schneider for an off-Broadway revival of the play at the Sheridan Square Playhouse in 1971.

In another note in preparation for drafting his complaint, Schneider reminds himself, 'I didn't change my mind [about continuing with the play]. He asked me to leave [the show], I refused' (UCSD, Alan Schneider Papers, MSS 103, Box 10, Folder 19). Schneider outlines his breach of contract suit against Myerberg in a detailed supplement to the arbitration hearing. He noted on 28 February 1957, the day after the first arbitration hearing, that there never was a Miami production per se but always only a New York production. The aim was always to open in New York:

> [I]ndeed we were as a company not happy to be trying the show out in Florida and would not have gone at all had it not been for Myerberg's [financial] guarantee there. So in my understanding the question of 'any other company' [theatrical phrasing in Schneider's contract that was subject of legal dispute

to the effect that Schneider be given the opportunity to direct 'any other company', which] meant that no matter what happened in Florida I would be given the opportunity of continuing with the play. (UCSD, Alan Schneider Papers, MSS 103, Box 10, Folder 19)

Alan Levy characterises the Miami production thus: 'The cast of five was paid off and disbanded' (Levy, 1956, 33). Myerberg, in turn, was telling a very different story to Beckett, or at least he was telling his version of the conflict and thereby drawing Beckett into this acrimonious dispute. Beckett summarised his exchange with Myerberg to his American publisher noting that

> Myerberg also told me, and this I forgot to put in the letter to Albery, that he might also lose Schneider who would perhaps have to go off on another project. I asked about replacing Schneider and he was very vague on that point. Myerberg says that he could not go on with his tour because the cast faded away. Pozzo got sick, Lucky was not able to go on at all, even at the first performance, and Ewell, says Myerberg, was hysterical and impossible to control. And so it goes. (Letter not included in *The Letters of Samuel Beckett*; see SULSC, Box 104)

Myerberg's version of events is not without merit, however, as Schneider admits in his written statement of 28 February 1957, which lays out communication technicalities:

> Mr. Myerberg says, he asked me on Jan. 19 [that is, after the Miami closing] to direct the New York version of *Godot* scheduled for spring, 1956, and I refused because I was busy elsewhere, why did he not then ask me again in writing – as prescribed in the contract – so that I would have an opportunity to say NO in writing, and thus free him from any subsequent claims on my behalf. Surely he would have thought of this. I continue to state that no such offer was made to me, either on January 19 or at any time. (UCSD, Alan Schneider Papers, MSS 103, Box 10, Folder 19)

Item 3 in Schneider's letter contract states: 'Your exclusive personal services shall commence on the first day of rehearsals and shall continue consecutively thereafter until the opening of the Play', with an autograph addition initialled by both Schneider and Myerberg that states, 'in New York'. Item 9 deals with

> other companies [that] are formed by me under my management [. . .] I agree to give you promptly Thirty (30) days' written notice of such formation, and you shall have the sole option to direct said company or companies [. . .]. You agree to exercise such option in writing within seven (7) days. (UCSD, Alan Schneider Papers, MSS 103, Box 10, Folder 19)

Myerberg did, however, officially enter a memorandum into arbitration evidence, a document in which he testified that such an offer was made.

Schneider further responded to Myerberg's accusation that he mistreated the actors and reduced them to tears. The principal issue was with J. Scott 'Jack' Smart (Pozzo), who indeed, as Myerberg related the story to Beckett, 'was not able to go on at all', or, as Schneider cites in arbitration, who 'broke down' and had to be hastily replaced by his understudy, John Paul. Myerberg additionally contended that Paul was inadequately prepared to assume the role of Lucky. Schneider does indeed acknowledge 'my part' in what he calls the actor's 'psychological difficulties' and cites the actor's weaknesses (UCSD, Alan Schneider Papers, MSS 103, Box 10, Folder 19). Schneider admits to additional difficulties with Charles Waldman (Lucky), whom he tried to discharge, but Myerberg insisted he stay for at least half the performances. In short, such issues of questionable directorial behaviour and inadequate professional performance reach far beyond the economic squabble. Bianchini's focus is on the disputed late revisions to the director's contract. Those dealt mostly with housing and per diem payments for the new venue in Florida but not the New York addendum as previously noted. She relies on the testimony of Schneider's agent, Audrey Wood, supporting Schneider's claim 'that he was never compensated appropriately for his work in Miami' (Bianchini, 2015, 36). But this finally is a minor issue in the overall dispute. The key financial issue in the litigation was the producer's continuing contractual obligations due the director for the New York production – even though he did not direct it.

Myerberg's defence of Schneider's dismissal was based on professional incompetence, that is, Schneider's 'failure to perform', and other contract violations – such personal posturing and legal wrangling that are too often endemic to professional theatre – and Beckett again found himself drawn into the midst of it. Beckett's allegiance would finally remain with his American publisher, who had his own ongoing contractual scuffles with Myerberg, and Rosset, in turn, would remain a strong supporter of and advocate for the Miami director.

Schneider would win his case against Myerberg, but the payout was essentially insignificant and the fees incurred through the process made it something of a Pyrrhic victory, 20 per cent for legal costs, fees to the American Arbitration Association, and for messenger services, photostats, and the like. In turn, however, he would go on to build his relationship with both Rosset and Beckett to become Beckett's premier American director. The focus here, however, is with the first of Beckett's plays to be staged in the United States, and it is revisionist in spirit, that the economically driven Myerberg, with all his faults and secretive, interventionist, and obstructionist tactics, made the decision to discharge Schneider and may, thereby, have rescued at least the Broadway production of *Godot* as he and his newly appointed Broadway director, Herbert Berghof, returned to Beckett's text as written. Van Hulle and Verhulst report that Berghof's and Lahr's texts remain on deposit at the New York Public Library (Performing Arts Research Collection, Berghof, Box 61, Folders 2 and 3, T-MSS 2010–106; Lahr RM 6961B). These are annotated copies of the 1954 Grove Press edition and were the scripts used for the 1956 production of the play at the John Golden Theater in New York (Van Hulle and Verhulst, 2018, 161), although Van Hulle and Verhulst confuse the date of production with the play's publication date: 'Director Herbert Berghof's promptbook, used for the 1954 John Golden Theater production in New York' (Van Hulle and Verhulst, 2018, 164). The more discerning of the New York theatre critics, however, still took issue with the Myerberg–Berghof staging, particularly over its treatment of Beckett's text. *Village Voice* critic Jerry Tallmer wrote on 26 April 1956,

> Its production in America is another extremely significant event, and I am glad that it has happened. But the play as produced by Michael Myerberg on Broadway is not the play as written in Paris by Beckett, or as read by me, at any rate, here in New York. [. . .] You will see a play wrongly accented into comic neorealism, wrongly loaded (in violence to the printed text) with comic 'business,' wrongly milked for every surface effect at the expense of the plumbless depths beneath. [. . .] It is doubtless going to be a long time before 'Godot' gets the American production that's really coming to it, and master-pieces come along very seldom more than once in a lifetime. (Tallmer, 1956)

For Tallmer, even with Schneider sidelined, Myerberg, Berghof, and Lahr, an actor who made much of his performing reputation on spontaneity and impro-visation, were still running roughshod over Beckett's text.

As interesting as the formal public documents prepared by Schneider and his attorney is a set of scraggly notes Schneider made in preparation for the lawsuit. For one, he makes reference to how the Florida production was advertised or merchandised and suggested a parallel between the ill-fated Miami venture and an earlier, similar, UK failure, '*Godot* in Blackpool', the 1956 touring produc-tion of *Waiting for Godot* that played at the Grand Theatre, and was, as David Kynaston puts it, 'entertaining the sticks' (Kynaston, 2010, 644). Like Miami, Blackpool is a resort and beach town and a haven for retirees or OAPs where the publicity for *Waiting for Godot* also generated unrealistic expectations, and so 'a large body of the audience' walked out each night. Kynaston summarises opening night in his history of the period:

> Week three of a testing tour that frayed the nerves of all concerned was at Britain's premier seaside resort. Advertised as 'inimitable' and 'priceless', Beckett's play arrived at the Grand Theatre, Blackpool, on Monday, June 4, to find itself up against stiff competition: The *Dave King Show* at the Winter Gardens Pavilion, Albert Modley (supported by Mike and Bernie Winters) starring in *Summer Showboat* at the Palace Theatre, and, twice nightly at the

Central Pier, *Let's Have Fun* with Jimmy James, Ken Dodd, and Jimmy
Clitheroe. It proved to be, according to the local newspaper, 'one of the
stormiest receptions in the theatrical history of Blackpool' as a large body of
the audience beat a disorganized retreat from the auditorium, others stayed and
displaying appalling manners made interjections that must have been audible to
those on the stage [. . .] and according to [Peter] Bull's account fewer than 100
altogether of the audience were left at the end, having started at some 700.
(Kynaston, 2010, 644)

The Edinburgh stop at the Royal Lyceum Theatre, a one-week tour beginning on
23 July 1956, likewise carried the following boilerplate programme note: '*The
most discussed play in London / Following its success at the Criterion Theatre*'.
'Success' here is defined chiefly in economic terms, since critics were not only
split but sharply divided in London, but sales were finally, after a slow start at
the Arts, robust:

[W]hen John Fowles tried to see it nine days after [the critic Anthony] Heap
[roundly condemned it, calling it 'a piece of highbrow-poppycock' and 'a
crashing, exasperating bore'] on the grounds that 'everyone goes, so we
must', he found that 'there were no seats for three weeks'. (Kynaston,
2010, 517)

That was not, needless to say, the Miami experience.

4 Cutting up *Godot*

For an author so reputedly meticulous, protective, even obsessive about the
publication and performance of his work, Beckett would be subject to any
number of clandestine 'improvements', creative reshaping and other non-
authorial interventions into his playscripts, the three words that the producer
Kenneth Tynan introduced into Beckett's minimalist playlet called 'Breath' in
1969 perhaps the most notorious. To Beckett's 'Stage littered with miscellan-
eous rubbish', Tynan added a simple participial phrase, 'including naked
bodies'. Leading off with Beckett's 'Breath', Tynan's sextravaganza, *Oh!
Calcutta!*, would premiere at the Eden Theater in New York City on
17 June 1969, and Tynan's intervention would contribute to what became
Beckett's greatest theatrical success. After a cautious opening with thirty-nine
previews, *Oh! Calcutta!* moved to Broadway's Belasco Theater on
26 February 1971 where it ran, and ran, and ran, with only slight interruption,
until 6 August 1989. Finally, 85 million people saw 1,314 performances,[16]
making it, uncontestedly, the most viewed Beckett play ever, a record unlikely

---

[16] See *Oh! Calcutta!* in Wikipedia: https://en.wikipedia.org/wiki/Oh!_Calcutta!

to be broken, although on advice from his American publisher Beckett withdrew his permission for further performances as soon as he legally could.

Such interventions as Tynan's were not as uncommon as one might expect given Beckett's reputation for fastidious oversight. Tynan's alteration to the play's set description was clandestine and his motives dissimilar from those of the Lord Chamberlain whose excisions were mandated in the name of modesty and decorum rather than to accentuate the lurid. All, however, modest or immodest, were part of the Anglo-American commercial theatre machinery and, in Tynan's case, reflected the radical change in social mores of the time. In the case of the Lord Chamberlain's office, its team of rewriters was following the charge of the office to sanitise those features of any public, dramatic performance that might offend the most delicate and sensitive members of the British public. Tynan's spirit was dominantly commercial within the contemporary political spirit of cultural revolution.

Less obvious and all but unacknowledged, the culprit of textual corruption could merely be chance, or rather ineptitude, the fumblings of ill-trained, inattentive editors or other functionaries in the publishing process. After the publication of *Waiting for Godot* in the United States, Grove Press sanctioned its republication by the major theatre journal of the day, *Theatre Arts*, successor to *Theatre Arts Monthly*, which routinely published playscripts of works performed on Broadway, especially those of American theatrical luminaries like Tennessee Williams, William Inge, and Arthur Miller. The American publisher Barney Rosset would write to Beckett on 8 March 1956 to inform him that *Theatre Arts* magazine requested to 'reprint the whole thing' (Beckett, 2011, 609n10), the request coming before the Broadway opening but well after the play's publication. Beckett's handwritten addendum of 15 March in response to Rosset was less than fully supportive: 'I am not sure that an integral publication in *Theatre Arts* magazine would help your sales. But I leave it to you to do what you judge best' (Beckett, 2011, 608). *Godot* would appear in the August 1956 issue, after the Broadway production had closed, the show running only some fifty-six performances between 19 April and 9 June. Of the publication, the annotators of the Beckett letters comment, almost offhandedly, certainly imprecisely, that 'although consecutively numbered, the order of the pages is incorrect in this publication' (Beckett, 2011, 609). More to the point, the *Theatre Arts* version was a publishing travesty even as its copy was set from the published Grove edition and not from the many reproduced versions from duplicating services. In New York, for example, Beckett's first translation of the play was reproduced by Hart Stenographic Bureau, a service, like the more famous Studio Duplicating Services, also of New York, used for legal depositions but also by many Broadway producers as a typing and duplicating service. The New York mimeographed version is nearly identical to the text submitted to the Lord Chamberlain's office for approval, but its pagination differs from those copies reproduced in London, and the American mimeograph varies significantly from the version subsequently revised and published by Grove Press in 1954. It is in that Grove Press revision that Beckett introduces what will become the play's most contested line, 'The mother had the clap'. The *Theatre Arts* publication was another resetting of the text by the magazine to comply with its own format, which included some twelve production photographs from both British and American stagings around which the play's text had to be arranged. This text for resetting would lack pagination since final pagination would need to await its positioning in the layout for this particular issue. Somewhere in that resetting process some functionary at the magazine must have dropped the loose sheets of unpaginated typescript since the pages got scrambled, badly, and, apparently, no one thought to recheck the now scrambled magazine version against the published book, which was readily available at the time (since September 1954) and from which the magazine's typescript was made. This accidentally reshuffled or cut-up version of the play was then printed, as scrambled, and was very widely read. The playscript was accompanied by Alan Levy's essay that included interviews with the producer Myerberg and the director Schneider, 'The LONG wait for godot' (Levy, 1956, 20–35, 96).

The *Theatre Arts* version faithfully follows the Grove text until page 45 (Beckett, 1956c, 37–45), where it then jumps to the ending of Act I (Beckett, 1956c, 46; Beckett, 1954, 35). Act I has no Boy at all, but he appears twice in Act II (Beckett, 1956c, 49, 61), as do Pozzo and Lucky. Lucky's tirade is now in Act II (Beckett, 1956c, 47–8), when Pozzo is apparently blind and Lucky presumably dumb and thereby censored, but they are sighted and loquacious, respectively, in something of, presumably, a medical miracle. Page 46 ends with Vladimir's line cut in mid-sentence, 'But it's the way of doing it that counts, the'; page 47 picks up with Estragon's 'I couldn't accept less' (Beckett, 1954, 26). None of the magazine's proofreaders apparently thought such a curious inconsistency between pages 46 and 47 was odd, or perhaps no more odd than a rambling, loquacious Lucky going dumb mid-act, or the mysterious affliction of a fully sighted Pozzo suddenly going blind before our eyes, or, rather, all these disjunctions were no more odd and irrational than other perceived non sequiturs in the play.

Even Alan Levy, who saw the play in Paris and New York and wrote the introductory essay to this edition, did not read the play in proof copy along with that for his essay since his summary contradicts the text of the play as it appears in the same magazine: 'Only two passers-by interrupt this morbid, two-man soliloquy. They come on in each act'; and 'At the end of the first act, a messenger tells the tramps that Godot will not come tonight' (Levy, 1956, 33). Well, not in this version as Levy's summary bears little relation to the text that follows. Each of those events Levy describes happens now in Act II as Pozzo appears suddenly early in the second act (Beckett, 1956c, 47) as does the boy's first appearance (49–50). Pozzo reappears without preliminaries on page 51, after the boy leaves, and they discuss emoluments. Page 54 then picks up from page 46. Pozzo and Lucky re-enter on page 56, the boy on page 61. And Levy himself emphasised what he sees as the play's irrationality and so misses the mark with his own critical assessment: 'It is a stammering, non-sensical and pathetic tirade that Lucky issues' (Levy, 1956, 33). Today we would call such a statement uninformed, although it still appears in print on occasion. As notably, if not as astonishingly, none of the magazine's readers commented on the confusions in the 'Letters' section of subsequent issues. Beckett, furthermore, certainly did not read proofs for this publication, nor, presumably, did anyone knowledgeable at Grove Press. The result is a wildly aberrant text, but one presumably read at the time by more magazine sub-scribers than customers reading the official Grove Press edition on sale at the theatre or in the few bookshops that carried the play. The result is a cut-up re-rendering of *Waiting for Godot*, something of a *Waiting Godot for* or *For Godot Waiting*, and, amid the reshuffle, something of a new text emerges, but, alas, yet another bad *Godot*.

A second curiosity was also part of the American publicity drive as the play found its way into the economically driven theatrical promotional machinery, one, again, that Rosset and Beckett agreed: a reduced and summarised version of the play published in the yearly *Best Plays* series edited by Louis Kronenberger. As Rosset wrote to Beckett on 8 May 1957:

> Enclosed are two reviews and a check for $100, which represents 50 per cent of a fee for condensation of *Godot* which was published by Dodd, Mead (along with several other plays) in a volume entitled *Best Plays* (for the 1955–1956 season). (see SULSC, Box 104)

In his introduction, Kronenberger declares *Waiting for Godot* 'a kind of philo-sophical quiz show' that offers 'storytelling without story', noting further that Beckett 'exhibits a genuine but essentially minor talent' (Beckett, 1956b, 13). When Kronenberger searches for analogies to try to situate *Godot* in a literary context for his readers, he turns to 'Henry James' *Turn of the Screw*, Kafka's *The Castle*, Pirandello's *Right You Are*, and Wilder's *The Skin of Our Teeth*' (Beckett, 1956b, 13). Levy, it turns out, uses the identical touchstones, leaving off only Pirandello (Beckett, 1956c, 34). For our purposes, the most intriguing

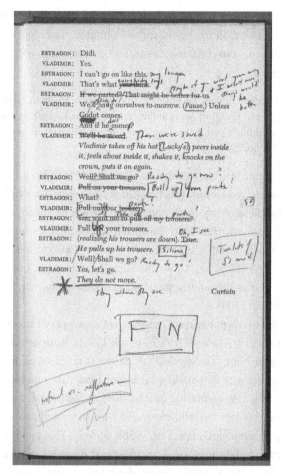

Figure 2 Alan Schneider's published copy of the American edition of *Waiting for Godot* with Thornton Wilder's dictated translation of the play.

of these analogies is with Wilder and his most recent Broadway success. Wilder was an inveterate adapter and spent considerable creative energy rewriting other authors, Joyce and Sartre among them. In this condensed *Godot*, the play is again cut up, with snippets of Beckett's dialogue interwoven with editorial summaries by other hands, essentially, at this point, co-authors who at times include additional bits of dialogue (Beckett, 1956b, 295–317).

Summaries are never neutral, of course, and here we find some twenty-three of them, some short, some quite extended, interspersed with dialogue. They shape our relation to and understanding of, in this case, Beckett's play:

> While Estragon continues his struggle with his boot, Vladimir riles him by asking if it hurts. Howls of anger at this lack of sympathy are met with equal anger on Vladimir's part that his own suffering is never taken into account. (Beckett, 1956b, 296)

And later, 'Vladimir is in a rage to leave' (Beckett, 1956b, 301). Lucky is called 'A creature of sorts', and we are told that 'Lucky responds like a tired old trained dog' (300). Needless to say, such phrases as 'Howls of anger' and 'Vladimir [...] in a rage' are not Beckett's. Too often the summaries tend to echo the New York production rather than Beckett's script. One can almost hear Bert Lahr's 'Howls' in echo of his 'Cowardly Lion' performance. Lucky's screed is cut roughly in half as the commentator notes dismissively, 'On and on and on goes the recitation' (304).

One high point of this publication, however, is the two-page cartoon by the noted Broadway caricaturist Al Hirschfeld, in which Lahr's Estragon looks decidedly Lahrish, of course, but E. G. Marshall's Vladimir is rendered as an echo of Stan Laurel. As interesting is Hirschfeld's casting of Lucky as a messianic figure on a distant hill declaiming something of a Sermon on the Mount, but the performance, in this case, is into the wilderness and without an audience as his back is turned to the play's principals (Beckett, 1956b, 306–7). That image offers a pithy visual interpretation of the play with Lucky's screed, his prophetic warnings, as the play's central feature, the dramatic climax of Act I. We might expect Act II to build on that moment in something of a traditional dramatic structure. Instead, his return in Act II turns out to be anticlimactic, deflationary even, and so a confirmation of Lucky's Act I decree that all humanity 'wastes and pines'. Such an image also belies some of the most common readings of the play, that nothing happens. Hirschfeld's image alone, with its hidden inscriptions of his daughter Nina's name (in Pozzo's trouser cuffs), is worth the price of the book on the aftermarket.

5 Transatlantic Parallels and Contrasts

On the other side of the Atlantic, Beckett's theatrical experience bore striking similarities to that which would develop in the United States. *Ulysses*, *Lolita*, and *Naked Lunch* could be officially banned in the United States, of course, as could, potentially, Beckett's novels, but historically Broadway has remained free of official restrictions even during the heyday of Burlesque. Neither Albery nor Myerberg had to contend with a figure who or agency that could restrict, alter, or quash a production by refusing a licence to perform. American producers needed no performance licences. But much commercial theatrical machinery on both sides of the Atlantic was not dissimilar, and the need for sample, promotional, and working copies of theatre pieces – in this case Beckett's play – for the business of theatre led to some initial textual variation. And the spirit of commercial theatre on both sides of the Atlantic entailed limiting an author's involvement, although Myerberg made some attempts to draw the author of *Godot* into the process. The US and UK productions were less simultaneous than dovetailed as the Arts Theatre production would run its course (opening 3 August 1955) well before the 3 January 1956 Miami opening, but the more commercial West End production, opening 12 September 1955, would begin before and continue for nearly two months beyond the Miami closing, completing its run by 24 March 1956. The New York opening would begin shortly after the London closing, on 19 April 1956, and run some sixty performances, until 9 June 1956. The complete and uncensored Grove Press edition of the play would be available from September 1954, but Faber & Faber's self-acknowledged 'timid' edition would appear in 1956, at the tail end of the London run. Hall's cast then might have worked with the Grove Press edition, and Peter Snow's mimeographed copy of the play gestured in that direction, but finally the British team worked exclusively with mimeographed copies, one of which was submitted to and is held in the Lord Chamberlain's archives now in the British Library (LCP/ 1954, i.e., submitted 1 July 1954, eleven months before the Arts opening); the British Library calls its copy 'the rehearsal script'.[17] Such reproduced versions were in circulation in both the United States and the United Kingdom, and an unannotated, separately typed, unnumbered, mimeographed copy of the US version is on deposit at The Ohio State University (Spec Rare CMS 53 726 and Figure 3), one not attributable to any production-related figure. These mimeographed duplicates remained in circulation even as Beckett subsequently made what he would deem his 'definitive' translation revisions for Grove Press (Beckett, 2011, 432; Rosset, 2016, 120), the text of which was available, at least in page proofs, after some printing delays, from May 1954, although official publication was delayed until autumn at Beckett's request.

Beckett admittedly deemed his original translations of 1953 hasty and insufficient; he subsequently 'improved' this earlier version, and he would propose

---

[17] See 'Censored Script of *Waiting for Godot* by Samuel Beckett', British Library: www.bl.uk/collection-items/censored-script-of-waiting-for-godot-by-samuel-beckett

```
                    LUCKY (Cont'd)
and Conard it is established as hereinafter but not so fast
for reasons unknown that as a result of the public works of
Puncher and Wattmann it is established as clearly so clearly
that in view of the labours of Fartov and Belcher unfinished
unfinished for reasons unknown of Testew and Conard un-
finished unfinished it is established what many deny that man
in Possy of Testew and Conard that man in short that man in
brief in spite of the progress of alimentation and defecation
wastes and pines wastes and pines and concurrently simultan-
eously for reasons unknown in spite of the strides of physical
culture the practice of sports such as tennis football running
cycling swimming riding flying conating tennis camogie skat-
ing of all kinds tennis flying sports of all sorts autumn
summer winter winter tennis of all kinds hockey of all sorts
penicilline and succedanea in a word I resume and concurrent-
ly simultaneously for reasons unknown to shrink and dwindle
in spite of the tennis I resume flying golf over nine holes
and eighteen tennis of all sorts in a word for reasons un-
known in Feckham Peckham Fulham Clapham namely concurrently
simultaneously for reasons unknown but time will tell to
dwindle dwindle I resume Fulham Clapham in a word the dead
loss per capitem since the death of Samuel Johnson being to
the tune of one inch four ounce per capitem approximately by
and large more or less to the nearest decimal good measure
round figures stark naked in the stockinged feet in Alabama
for reasons unknown in a word no matter what matter the facts
are there and considering what is more what is still more
hrave that it appears what is still more grave that in the
light of the labours in progress of Steinweg and Peterman
it appears what is still more grave that in the light the
light the light of the labours abandoned of Steinweg and
Peterman that in the plains in the mountains by the seas by
the rivers of water and fire the air is the same and the
earth namely the air and the earth in the great cold the
air and the earth abode of stones in the great cold alas alas
in the year of their Lord six hundred something the air the
earth the sea the earth abode of stones in the great deeps
the great cold on sea on land and in the air I resume for
reasons unknown in spite of the tennis the facts are there
but time will tell I resume alas alas on on in short in fine
on on abode of stones who can doubt it I resume but not so
fast I resume the skull to shrink pine waste and concurrently
simultaneously for reasons unknown in spite of the tennis
on on the beard the flames the tears the stones so blue so
calm alas alas on on the skull the skull the skull the skull
in Alabama in spite of the tennis the labours abandoned left
unfinished graver still abode of stones in a word I resume
alas alas abandoned unfinished the skull the skull in Alabama
in spite of the tennis the skull alas the stones Conard
              (melee, final vociferations)
tennis...the stones...so calm...Conard...unfinished...

                      POZZO
His hat!

         (VLADIMIR seizes Lucky's hat.  Silence of Lucky.
He falls.  Silence.  Panting of the victors)
```

Figure 3 Earliest English translation in mimeograph copy including Lucky's references to 'Conard', 'Samuel Johnson', and 'Alabama' with character names centred on the page.

With thanks to the Film and Playscript collection in the Rare Books and Manuscripts Library of The Ohio State University Libraries. Published with permission of Edward Beckett on behalf of the Samuel Beckett Estate.

that Faber & Faber publish that revised text in 1965. Beckett had denigrated his 'first version of *Godot*' to his American publisher on 25 June 1953:

This translation has been rushed, so that [original producer] Mr [Harold] ·
Oram may have something to work on as soon as possible, but I do not think

the final version will differ from it very much. I should like to know what date roughly you have in view for publication. (Beckett, 2011, 384–5)

The intermediary between Beckett and Oram was one Pamela Mitchell, who, in September 1953, acting as representative of Harold Oram, Incorporated, met with Beckett in Paris to negotiate the rights for the American premiere of *Waiting for Godot*. At this time, on 1 September 1953, Beckett responded to Rosset's suggestion that some Americanising of the text might be needed for US audiences. Beckett repeated his earlier assessment that the initial translation 'was done in great haste to facilitate the negotiations of Mr Oram and I do not myself regard it as very satisfactory', adding, 'But I have not yet had the courage to revise it' (Rosset 2016, 117; Beckett, 2011, 397). Myerberg may have taken his cue to have changes made to the text from Beckett's own denigration of his translation, but his most direct influence was Thornton Wilder, who would go on to produce at least a rough, more Americanised translation of the play for the Miami premiere. Van Hulle and Verhulst acknowledge that 'neither Beckett's holograph, nor his original typescript of this first draft [the unsatisfactory translation cited above] has been found' (Van Hulle and Verhulst, 2018, 269), but that provisional translation was quickly reproduced and widely circulated in both the United States and the United Kingdom in mimeographed format. Since no published version was yet available for producers at the time, directors and actors worked with such mimeographs as consultations and casting began and, in the UK, through rehearsals and performances. Schneider's promptbook copy is yet another retyping but of Beckett's revised translation, that is, the version published by Grove Press in 1954, which Wilder had read and in turn 'improved' substantially. One exception to the circulation of mimeographed copies was the typescript that Beckett sent to Dublin via his long-time friend A. J. 'Con' Leventhal slated for production at the Pike Theatre, which, like London's Arts Theatre, was a private theatre club and so, for the most part, functioned outside of the strict censorship restrictions of the Republic. Beckett wrote Leventhal on 17 November 1953: 'I have translated the text myself, pretty literally, and am now beginning to revise it for publication in New York next spring. [. . .] Shall send you the MS as soon as ready if you are interested in taking on this probably thankless job' (Beckett, 2011, 417), that is, of overseeing or at least reporting on the Dublin production in his absence. At Beckett's request, following Albery's preference, the Dublin opening was delayed a fortnight until after the (censored) London West End opening on 12 September 1955, and *Godot* would open in Dublin on 28 October 1955. The Dublin production, with Alan Simpson's own localised alterations, was essentially that of the Grove Press text. In anticipation of some

resistance, however, Simpson issued a warning to his audience since his production would be uncensored, the world premiere thus. In a warning that
appeared in the 'Irishman's Diary' column in the *Irish Times* on
20 October 1955, Simpson would essentially restate Beckett's warning to him
(Beckett, 2011, 418). In Simpson's words:

> The script of this play contains certain crudities. In deference to the wishes of
> the author and to preserve the artistic integrity of the piece it is being played
> unabridged in the Pike Theatre Club. While the directors would not presume
> to debar lady guests of members from admission, they would point out that
> they attend at the risk of being offended. (qtd in Murray, 1984, 103–4)

The textual and transmission requirements of copies of the play available for
distribution finally outpaced his ability to meet that demand: how many copies
he could or was willing to produce on his manual typewriter, how many times,
that is, he was willing to retype the entire play. What he sent Simpson via
Leventhal was a typescript copy with modifications, corrections, and revisions
in his hand, alterations that were made for the Grove Press publication and so
copied onto the Pike typescript (for full collation, see Dukes, 1995a, 80–91).
The Pike typescript then contains some key, now typed, revisions to Lucky's
speech made for Grove Press, including 'The loss per head since the death of
Bishop Berkeley', rather than 'the loss per capitem since the death of Samuel
Johnson' (as in OSU 51; 'per capita', Beckett, 1956a, 43 and Beckett, 1957, 30;
see also Federman and Fletcher, 1970, 78). And the site of primitive forms of
human or near-human life was altered from 'Alabama' to the similar-sounding
'Connemara', a last-minute revision that may have been made with an eye
towards the Irish market (see facsimile page in Van Hulle and Verhulst, 2018,
73); all five known mimeographed duplicates cite 'Alabama', the translation
made, as Beckett admitted, for the American producer Harold Oram and so with
the American market in mind – but 'Samuel Johnson' remains in all mimeographs (see, for example, Albery or Snow, I-41). This Pike Theatre typescript
that Van Hulle and Verhulst correctly call 'the second typescript of *Waiting for
Godot* (ETP, 39 r)', a 'dirty copy', as Beckett called it, and what Van Hulle and
Verhulst identify as 'a sibling' to the original, 1953 translation, is a step beyond
all the mimeograph versions (Van Hulle and Verhulst, 2018, 70).

That is, after the French production had closed at the end of October and the
play still unpublished in English, Beckett 'improved' his own early translation,
asking Rosset, on 14 December 1953, to delay publishing the original translation in favour of what Beckett will call a 'definitive' version:

> Could you possibly postpone setting the galleys until 1st week in January
> [1954], by which time you will have received the definitive text. I have made

a fair number of changes, particularly in Lucky's tirade, and a lot of correcting would be avoided if you could delay things for a few weeks. (Beckett, 2011, 432; Rosset 2016, 120)

Rosset agreed, and it would be this revised Grove Press text of 1954 that Beckett would subsequently recommend to his German publisher Siegfried Unseld on 4 June 1962 and to his English editor Charles Monteith on 13 January 1964. His 10 November 1962 letter to Unseld noted that the English could not stage the uncut text 'without running into trouble with the censors [. . .] they could not stage the uncut text as published by Grove Press, without once again submitting it for the Lord Chamberlain's approval. It is of course the Grove Press text which should have appeared in your [*Dramatische Dichtungen 1*] edition', instead of the Faber published text, which at the time was its sanitised 1956 version (Beckett, 2011, 581n2). Beckett would return to the issue on 15 November 1963, urging Monteith to reconsider publishing what he calls the 'integral' text of *Waiting for Godot* and lamenting the publication of the censored text in Suhrkamp's collected trilingual edition: 'The whole question was brought forcibly to my mind by the first volume just published of Suhrkamp's trilingual edition of my plays in which he has used quite unnecessarily your text instead of the integral one', replicating in the process Faber & Faber's bad *Godot* (Beckett, 2014, 580). In 1964, Beckett would propose to Monteith that 'The final Godot [*sic*] text I propose is the Grove Press text as corrected by me (black corrections, ignore red) with [American] spelling anglicized as necessary' (Faber, 2019, 279).

But even in the autumn of 1955, the Criterion transfer under way, Monteith had still not signed Beckett for Faber & Faber. Writing to Rosica Colin about the play on 9 September 1955, Monteith asked 'if the British rights were still available. This is simply to say that I am still interested in it and very much hope that you will let us have it on offer' (qtd in Faber, 2019, 236). Just over a month later, on 11 October 1955, Monteith wrote to thank the Colin editor Diana Pullein-Thompson for sending 'a copy of *Waiting for Godot* amended to meet the requirements of the Lord Chamberlain. We can now get on straight away with our production. As you know we want to bring out the book as soon as possible next year' (qtd in Faber, 2019, 236), as they did in February. Monteith apparently never questioned the nature of the emendations, nor their necessity for the purposes of publication. He simply accepted what was offered, apparently. Albery, or someone at the Colin agency, had already marked the objectionable portions of Beckett's play, presumably in one or another of the performance copies. If the latter were the case, the likely candidate, the one handling the *Waiting for Godot* transaction, was the woman to whom Monteith's letter was addressed, Diana Pullein-Thompson, who, although only at the agency for a short period, seems to have played a pivotal role in the publication of Beckett's first produced play in the United Kingdom. Pullein-Thompson would herself go on to become a bestselling author, part of what had become a family franchise of 'pony books'. Thus, the first text of *Waiting for Godot* that Monteith and the staff of Faber & Faber saw was a sanitised mimeographed copy.

By 15 November 1963, Monteith began preparations to publish the uncensored text as he wrote to Peter du Sautoy that the next group requesting to stage *Waiting for Godot* should reapply to the Lord Chamberlain for permission to stage the original version. If that request were successful, Faber & Faber would consider republishing the play in its uncensored form. To that end, Beckett sent copies of the Grove Press edition to Monteith, inscribed to him, indicating all the words to restore (Beckett, 2014, 581n3). By 13 January the following year, Beckett returned the corrected proofs of *Play* to Monteith, and he took the opportunity once again to lobby Faber & Faber on the issue of *Godot*, recommending again publication of the complete, 'integral' text:

> The final *Godot* text I propose is the Grove Press text corrected by me (black corrections, ignore red). The Lord Chamberlain's objections, as well as I can remember, were to button it, pubis, erection, clap, arse, piss, ballocksed and farted, pp. 8, 12, 15, 21, 38, 50 and 52 respectively of Grove edition. (qtd in Faber, 2019, 279)[18]

Beckett's letter was sent in reply to Monteith's request to establish what he called a 'canonical' script by comparing the Faber & Faber text to that supplied by Grove Press, and the colour distinctions referred to by Beckett address the collation of US and UK editions made by Monteith's secretary (full details in Van Hulle and Verhulst, 2018, 121–4). While preparations were under way at Faber & Faber to publish the uncensored text, the English Stage Company began its application to stage it, but that request would again be denied by the Lord Chamberlain. By 19 March 1964, a frustrated Beckett would advise Unseld that 'it is safer to use the American edition in all cases' (Beckett, 2014, 597).

Beckett's suggested publication of the Grove Press edition, if accepted by Monteith, would have avoided the current disparities among the principal English-language versions of *Godot*. That is, throughout the process of textual duplication, performance-driven alterations, and retranslation, Beckett himself made separate revisions for American and British publishers and so retained

---

[18] This crucial letter is not included in Beckett (2014), but the publication of the Grove Press text by Faber & Faber is proposed in Beckett's letter to Monteith of 15 November 1963 (Beckett, 2014, 580). Beckett continues to call the 1956 Faber & Faber edition 'the playing version authorized by the Lord Chamberlain', but it was not the text performed in London in 1955–6. Closer to the 'playing version', again, is the *Samuel French 'Acting Edition'*.

fundamental differences not only between French and English versions, beginning with their titles, of course, but also between what became, finally, separately revised texts for his English-language publishers. One fully revised,
'definitive' version, then, was finally published by Grove Press in the autumn
of 1954 in advance of all English-language productions, and he would create
a separate 'definitive' version for Faber & Faber in 1965.

At about the time of the recast Broadway opening at the John Golden Theater
on 19 April 1956, a new production in Myerberg's strategy, two years after the
play's publication by Grove Press and not long after the censored Faber & Faber
edition of February 1956 finally appeared, the textual issues surrounding
Beckett's first produced play were, to say the least, confused: eight decidedly
different English-language versions of *Godot* were in circulation and thus in or
available for performance. Many of these bore fingerprints other than those of
the author. A ninth was created for an uncensored performance at the Royal
Court Theatre in December of 1964, in anticipation of the revised Faber & Faber
text, finally published in January 1965 in which a 'Publisher's Note' informs
readers that the previous deletions of 1956 'have been restored in the text
printed here' and that 'this text has been authorized by Mr Beckett as definitive'.

In circulation, to one degree or another in 1957, however, were the following:

(1) Beckett's original (hasty) Glenville/Oram translation of May–June 1953,
    acknowledged to Rosset on 5 July 1953. Van Hulle and Verhulst note that
    Beckett would subsequently begin to revise this English translation in
    November 1953 (see their full calendar of translation in Van Hulle and
    Verhulst, 2018, 164).

(2) A pre-publication mimeograph reproduced in the United States by Oram/
    Myerberg, the sole known copy now at The Ohio State University (OSU).[19]
    Van Hulle and Verhulst, too, consider this version 'a copy of the script that
    Harold L. Oram had made in America on the basis of the first typescript' (Van
    Hulle and Verhulst, 2018, 67n24). This differs only in pagination and some
    stylistic features from those mimeographs duplicated in the United Kingdom
    (see Figure 3). Of what they refer to as 'OSUac', Van Hulle and Verhulst say
    that 'The Rare Books and Manuscripts Library at Ohio State University holds
    a playscript of *Waiting for Godot*, but it is unclear for which production this
    was used. There are no annotations' (Van Hulle and Verhulst, 2018, 164). The

---

[19] A copy of this American duplicated script is held at The Ohio State University Rare Books and
Special Collections library but neither in nor cross-referenced to the university's major Beckett
collection. My thanks to Professor Jennifer A. Buckley of the University of Iowa for calling my
attention to this holding and to Rebecca Jewett, Coordinator of Public Services & Operations,
University Libraries, Thompson Library Special Collections, The Ohio State University for
making it available, with the permission of Edward Beckett, whom I, likewise, thank.

copy referred to here, dated 1954 by OSU, so before any details of any American production were in place, was clearly generated for the American premiere, although used only for initial solicitations and never used in production since the improved Grove Press edition was available from September 1954, more than a year before Miami rehearsals began. The Ohio State University designates its copy as follows: 'SPEC RARE CMS 53 726 Waiting for Godot tragicomedy in two acts 1954' (page 1–18 missing and presumably lost). The pagination and format of character names differ from item (3) in this list in that the speakers' names are set in large capitals and centred on the page, so they appear above the dialogue. This is the sole version, printed or mimeographed, formatted thus. Beckett suggested a format to Rosset in a letter of 14 December 1954 as 'another possibility' to replace the initial Grove design (Rosset, 2016, 119–20); although that initial design is currently unknown it may have been the format of the OSU mimeograph. The OSU mimeograph contains an additional deviation from the other mimeographed copies (item (3) in the list) in that Beckett's note to 'Pozzo takes off his hat', 'All four wear bowlers', an extra-textual note that should come at the foot of the page, falls so in the OSU mimeograph, 1–38, but appears part way down the page in the British retypings (Albery/Snow, I-30); its point of reference is midway on I-29, so that the note, conventionally, should appear at the foot of that page. In Albery/Snow, the note appears to be neither a stage direction, since it is numbered, nor a footnote since it falls one-third of the way down the page. It appears as something of a textual intrusion in the UK-generated reproductions. Other minor differences include page designations in the Ohio State copy are all in Arabic numerals, act then page number within the act. In the UK reproductions, the act designation is Roman in Act I and Arabic in Act 2. Further, speeches continued onto the following page are indicated as a contraction 'Cont'd' in the Ohio State copy and as an abbreviation 'Contd.', with end stop, in Albery/Snow. The point of potential debate here is which of these duplications, item (2) or (3), preceded the other. The conclusion here is that the American retyping clearly came first.

(3) Mimeographed reproductions of the 1953 translation, made from but with alterations to item (1) or (2); of two Albery copies in Texas, one hand-numbered '25', the other 'copy numbered #53', according to Van Hulle and Verhulst, also bears a note in autograph, 'To be copied'. The handwritten number '25' suggests at least that number of duplicates, many more than Beckett could have produced on his typewriter. Van Hulle and Verhulst further suggest that 'The copy numbered #53 has a red cover and carries the note "To be copied" in the top left corner' (Van Hulle and Verhulst, 2018, 63), and they offer the following genealogy:

> This note ['To be copied'] leaves open the possibility that what Beckett
> sent Peter Glenville in early September 1953 was not in fact a copy of his
> first typescript ([ET1]), but a copy of the script that Harold L. Oram had
> made in America on the basis of the first typescript (see chapter 3.1).

Either 'possibility' would represent the same stage of translation, however.
Albery then would have his own copies reproduced in London. This 'red
cover' copy was apparently used at some point by the actor playing
Vladimir,[20] Richard Dare in London, and is revised, like Snow's copy, to
include most of Beckett's Grove Press revisions. Van Hulle and Verhulst
agree that the Ohio State copy (item (2) in the list) is that produced by Oram
in New York and precedes those in the Albery archive. The American and
British duplicated copies are almost textually identical in all but pagination
and certain typing conventions regarding speaker designations and footnote
placement. The 'To be copied' note, however, may merely signify a need
for further copies for rehearsals since that text is identical to the one sent to
the Lord Chamberlain's office for approval except for its cover.

Further, what Van Hulle and Verhulst read as the number 53 in the upper
right-hand corner of the cover, in a note even fainter than the 'To be copied'
inscription, may simply be the date of receipt rather than the copy number, as
the number 25 is, that is, '53 for 1953. To this reader's eyes, moreover, another
possibility emerges; '53' might be a set of initials, that is, 'SB', for example.
For one, if what might be seen as 'SB' were a number, its handwriting is
considerably different from the other clearly numbered copies, the number 15
on the Peter Snow copy, for instance, or the number 25 on the other Albery
copy. Its script, moreover, is close to that used for the 'To be copied' designation, so it may simply signify, 'To be copied [for] SB', a note that further
duplications are needed from the same stencil. The more likely possibility,
however, is that the 1953 text would need to be recopied subsequently once the

---

[20] Albery's actor's copy contains the following pencilled blocking notes for Vladimir's entrance in
Act II, as transcribed by the editorial team of the Beckett Digital Manuscript Project but
corrected as follows:

SIT
Hat
rest [or 'next' in my reading, that is, 'Hat next (to) tree' in viewing order]
tree
X W [or 'so' not 'W'] to leave [i.e., 'Cross so to leave']
Look off
X L
X C boots
Craddle [*recte* 'Cradle'] boot smell boot down tree

Lord Chamberlain has ruled on which portions of Beckett's play needed excision or alteration so that cast and crew had accurate performance scripts:

> That Beckett had received a copy of this script is evident from his letter to Barney Rosset of 1 September 1953 [hence the number 53, as suggested]: The copy made by the services of Mr Oram [they suggest a copy of item (2), the American retyping of item (1)] contains a number of mistakes' [Beckett, 2011, 397–8]. This letter precedes Beckett's note to Glenville by a week, so it is possible that Beckett was out of [carbon] copies of his own typescript and sent one of Oram's scripts [mimeographed duplicates] instead, knowing that it was only a preliminary version to help the British backers find a theatre. This copy may then have been further reproduced, which would not only explain the note 'To be copied' but also the absence of an original typescript from the papers of Glenville and Albery, which only contain the [mimeographed] playscript. Like Oram's copy, as Beckett told Rosset, this script and its siblings (ETLC and ET Snow) also contain a fair number of typos and mistakes. (Beckett, 2011, 397; Van Hulle and Verhulst, 2018, 67n24)

The 'To be copied' version does not follow the Oram/OSU formatting (see Figure 3), however, and so it seems to request further copies of the second mimeograph state. Another copy of this 'red cover' version of the script is in private hands, part of the collection of the visual artist and book collector Yuri Pattison. It is unannotated and so not associated with any production-related figure, but the number it bears, apparently '55', may be significant again not to designate the number copies made from a mimeograph stencil but the date of this new series of 'red cover' copies, this time for rehearsals in 1955, hence 55 or '55 (see Figure 4).

Figure 4 Cover detail of mimeograph copy in the possession of Yuri Pattison.

In fact, the opening page of Act II of the Pattison copy shows a decided weakening of type clarity, particularly in the 'o' of 'Two' and 'Same place' (see Figure 5). Such typographical lightening would seem unlikely if the Pattison mimeograph were only two copies away from the other 'red cover' copy numbered 53. More likely, the number 55 designates another round of copies made from the same stencil for the 1955 London rehearsals. This would suggest that of Beckett's original translation, two sets of mimeographs were made in 1953, one in the United States and one in the United Kingdom, and, further, another set of copies, with red covers, was made in 1955 prior to London

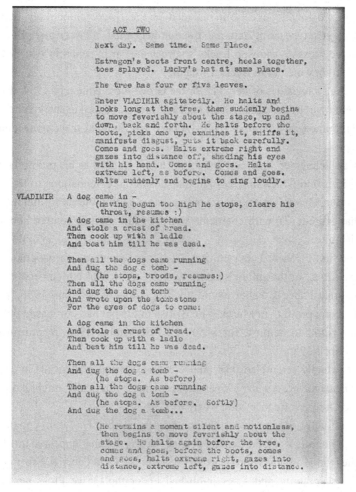

Figure 5 Page of Yuri Pattison copy showing some degradation of print quality at the opening of Act II.

rehearsals, and these would not yet include the Lord Chamberlain's decisions since that had not been finalised before the Arts Theatre production went into rehearsals, and would have been irrelevant for that 'theatre club' performance. Hence the 'red cover' mimeograph reproduction associated with Vladimir's role.

In this catalogue of script reproductions, the Ohio State mimeograph seems to be the anomaly, which may be why it does not appear in Van Hulle and Verhulst's 'Genetic Map' (Van Hulle and Verhulst, 2018, 166), which moves from Beckett's typescript, 'English TS1', to 'English Playscripts', the mimeographs produced in the United Kingdom. The contention here, and admittedly implied by Van Hulle and Verhulst, is that the Oram-generated Ohio State mimeograph retyped in New York and cited here as item (3) might have been included in the *Godot* chronology between Beckett's typescript and the London-generated 'Playscripts'. Beckett's Grove Press revisions to Lucky's speech appear in pencil in Albery I-41–2, but they are not in Beckett's hand.

(4) Beckett's revisions of item (1) for the Grove Press edition of 1954, deemed 'definitive' by the author; these revisions are reproduced in autograph to item (3), mimeograph number 25, by Albery and Snow in their mimeographed copies.

(5) Alan Schneider's retyped version of item (4); used as his promptbook of 1955/6 into which he recorded his substantial emendations to the script used in Miami; the text follows the Grove edition but its format matches that of item (2), with character names in full capitals centred above the dialogue.

(6) The first Faber & Faber edition, from a pre-censored mimeograph copy (by Albery or the author's agent, Rosica Colin). This edited version is the one that Faber & Faber would finally publish in February 1956, adding a second printing in March. The British publisher had purchased publication rights to item (4) for $150 by 24 September 1955, reconfirmed on 12 April 1956.

(7) A textually scrambled (essentially cut-up) reprint of item (4) in *Theatre Arts* magazine, August 1956, which, at least theoretically, might have been used for performance somewhere.

(8) And finally, in many ways the most egregious bad *Godot*, in competition with items (1)–(6), the *Samuel French 'Acting Edition'* appeared in 1957. It cites the 1954 uncensored Grove Press not the 1956 Faber & Faber edition as its authority and so is published under the Grove Press worldwide performance rights. That is, Grove's rights inside and outside the United States included all performances in English. The designation of 'Acting Edition' by Samuel French allowed it to be sold in competition with Grove

Press in the States and with Faber & Faber in the United Kingdom. The edition also cites a 1955 text with Beckett's copyright deemed 'unpub. 41144' (unpublished), a date also acknowledged in the Faber & Faber editions (Beckett, 1956a, 7):

'This play is copyright in 1955', but copyrighted not by Faber & Faber, which did not then hold the rights to publish the play, nor did it hold any performance rights – ever. This substantially modified Samuel French edition reflects the extensive rewritings made for both London productions, and this edition was sold throughout the United States, the United Kingdom, Australia, and Canada as noted on the copyright page. A transgressive, collaborative, co-authored text, it was finally replaced by the Faber & Faber's 'Revised Edition' of 1965 but only in 2004. In general, Samuel French does not record reprintings on its copyright page, so dating its various versions depends on factors like the introduction of ISBN numbers in the 1970s and barcodes in the 1980s.

Most curious, perhaps, is how such a renegade edition was published in the first place. On 15 May 1955, Beckett wrote to Rosset about a request for amateur rights to *Waiting for Godot*: 'Received an application from USA for the amateur rights, I suppose I shove it on to Kitty Black' (see SULSC, Box 104). Other requests evidently followed from amateur British theatre groups as well since, on 2 August 1956, writing for Rosica Colin, Ltd, Black proposed an 'acting edition' to Beckett because amateur theatre companies could not perform the British edition, she thought, since 'Faber published the complete text without the Lord Chamberlain's cuts'. Beckett corrected her on 10 August, rejecting the idea of an 'acting edition' out of hand:

> There is no need for a further 'acting edition' of <u>Godot</u>. Faber and Faber did <u>not</u> publish the complete text (my grievance). Their edition respects all the LC [Lord Chamberlain] cuts. Their text is the text used in the Criterion production and their edition is the 'acting edition'. (Beckett, 2011, 645)

Beckett here, in turn, seems 'not correctly informed' and further seems unaware of the extent that the text used for the Arts and Criterion productions had been altered, enhanced, or embellished even beyond the alterations to, or what he called errors in, the text that Oram had duplicated in the United States (Beckett, 2011, 397–8). He had, moreover, seen the London production multiple times with Schneider as he wrote to Pamela Mitchel on 16 December:

> I am just back from a rather hectic time in London. I went there with Alan Schneider, director of American production, to work with him, and we did so, I think to some purpose. [. . .] The play is doing well at the Criterion, Piccadilly, and we had a great party in the theatre for its 100th there, buckets of champagne

and a powerful crowd. They were all very nice to me in London, critics and journalists included, they left me alone. (Beckett, 2011, 582–3)

Rosica Colin and Curtis Brown seem to have worked around Beckett's objections in responding to requests from Grove Press that an edition for amateurs was needed to meet the demand for an 'acting edition', so contracts were issued for such apparently based, at least for copyright purposes, on the Grove Press text of 1954 and Grove's world performance rights. That 'acting edition' was published in 1957 as the *Samuel French 'Acting Edition'* through Grove Press, which was, as Beckett confirmed in October 1955, 'proprietor of translation'. Van Hulle and Verhulst do some deep digging to turn up a key piece in this publication puzzle, a letter of 14 August 1956 from Kitty Black to Jérôme Lindon announcing that such a deal had been completed. It offers yet another instance of economic forces working independent of the author:

> I am enclosing a copy of an 'acting edition' as prepared by Samuel French. From this you will see that the cost, lay-out and information contained is quite different from that contained in the 'reading edition' as published by Fabers. This type of publication is that habitually used by amateurs, and they are usually very unhappy at having to work from anything unfamiliar. With regard to the text, I understand that the cuts demanded by the Lord Chamberlain were incorporated in the Faber edition, so that it would be this text that would be used. There is no question of making any further alterations to the text. (Institut Mémoires de l'édition contemporaine (IMEC), Fonds Samuel Beckett, Boîte 5, Correspondance 1953–1957, qtd in Van Hulle and Verhulst, 2018, 116–17)

But what 'would be this text that would be used' in the Samuel French edition was not 'the Faber edition', as Black assumed. The edition also bears the copyright '© Acting Edition by Samuel Beckett 1957'. The phrasing, presumably, separates the Samuel French edition from that published by Faber & Faber the previous year, but such a copyright assignation also suggests Beckett's approval of this edition. As it turns out, it seems incontestable that no one at Grove Press, certainly not Rosset or his literary staff, and presumably no one at Rosica Colin and Curtis Brown had any inkling of what Samuel French had published, even as Black had a copy of the text which she passed on to Lindon but certainly not to Beckett. Samuel French did not reprint the Grove Press text of 1954, as one might expect given the copyright date, nor did it print the Faber & Faber text of the year before but printed, doubtless with the best of intentions, the substantially altered, amplified, or rewritten Peter Hall script bearing scant resemblance to the uncensored American edition. It was, however, the text acted, thus an 'acting edition', performed on the London stage.

Samuel French makes no mention of the Faber & Faber edition of 1956 on its copyright page, but Faber & Faber, on the other hand, does include a separate

'Note', '*This play is copyright in* 1955', an acknowledgement of performance rights for the United Kingdom held through Curtis Brown for Grove Press. Those contracts are held in the Syracuse University Grove Press archives (SULSC, Box 106, 'Rights and permissions, Amateur productions 1956–1971 [2 folders]').

The curious authorisation of the *Samuel French 'Acting Edition'* of *Godot* would not be the only time that the commercial machinery of theatre and Beckett's publishers and literary agents were not in total accord with the author's wishes.[21] On 8 April 1959, Beckett wrote to Rosset complaining of an unauthorised publication of his early and suppressed short story *First Love* about which he notes, 'I am absolutely opposed to the publication of this text or to its circulation in any form outside Bosquet's class' at Brandeis University where Beckett authorised its classroom use. In an addendum to that notification of piracy, Beckett adds 'More heartening news' that includes another instance of his losing control over his literary output, or rather that his literary agents had authorised productions that he wished prohibited:

> More heartening news. When the organisers of the Dublin Dramatic Festival 1958 knuckled under to their Archbishop Quaid and accepted his veto on Joyce and O'Casey I withdrew *Endgame* and the Mime which the Pike theatre was to have done and decided I didn't want my plays to be performed in Eire in the future. Now I learn that some group I never heard of, having announced in an evening paper they had succeeded in 'talking me round' (never had sight or sound of any of them), are doing *Endgame* AND *Krapp* in a Dublin theatre, Curtis Brown having gaily given them the rights without consulting me, though they should have known from their ex-employee Kitty Black what the situation was. Result: a letter from the Pike wounded to the heart (naturally). I tried to stop the production. Impossible. Lovely life the literary. (This telling letter is not included in *The Letters of Samuel Beckett*; see SULSC, Box 104)

The Lord Chamberlain's archive also contains an anomalous edition of the play, which might be a number 9 in this catalogue, although it appears in 1964. An unpublished mock-up by the English Stage Company, not in the Faber & Faber format despite its inclusion of Faber copyright dates, was created by the English State Company using its own theatrical house style and pagination for its duplicates and following the format of the Oram and Albery mimeographs.[22] Unlike earlier mimeographs, however, this version includes Faber & Faber copyright information as if it were already published in the United Kingdom and this version was submitted to the Lord Chamberlain's office on 1 December 1964 in anticipation

---

[21] Details of this and other contractual transactions are also available in the Barney Rosset Papers at Columbia University, MSS 1543 as 'Misc Rights Requests', 1955–97 (2 folders) in Box 52 Folder 16–17.

[22] This mimeograph version is also paginated thus: I-2–I-59; 2-2–2-52; I-1 and 2-1 unpaginated.

of an uncensored performance at the Royal Court Theatre at the end of that month. In a letter to the Lord Chamberlain of 17 December 1964, Royal Court Artistic Director Anthony Page emphasised that 'I am directing "Waiting for Godot" and am working with Mr. Beckett who is here for rehearsals'. That performance was to coincide with Faber & Faber's release of an uncensored, complete edition of the play the following year that would be sold, then, during the run of the revival. But the copyright ruse, the invocation of Beckett's presence at rehearsals, and the anticipated publication of a new edition held little sway with the Lord Chamberlain. Federman and Fletcher claim that 'The complete and unexpurgated text [was] first performed publicly in Great Britain at the Royal Court Theatre, London, on 30 December 1964, directed by Anthony Page, assisted by the author' (Federman and Fletcher, 1970, 78). That did not happen. The Lord Chamberlain's blue pencil reinstated the Criterion cuts of 1954/5, missing, however, 'The mother had the clap' (LCP 1964/51, p. I-18) and marking for additional deletion 'The Hard Stool' that was never at issue in the 1954/5 deletion requests (LCP 1964/51, p. I-40). Such textual mitigation at which Monteith would suggest to Beckett in 1957 seems to have led to preparations to issue such an uncensored text in 1959, but that turned out to be only a 'paper covered' reprint of the 1956 edition, reprinted again in 1962. The unexpurgated text would emerge in print in hard and soft covers only in 1965 and that in anticipation of an unexpurgated performance that did not occur. In his report for the Lord Chamberlain dated 4 December for performances scheduled to open on 30 December 1964 (and stamped 24 December), an exasperated C. D. Heriot made clear the continuation of performance restrictions to Anthony Page (for further details, see Gontarski, 2018, 60):[23]

> All the cuts made in the original have been restored [that is, they remain in effect] and at least one new one [has been added]. This I have listed together with two warnings based on the complaint received from Lady Howitt (File no. 440/55) [these principally against miming or simulating urination, or as she put it in her letter of complaint, that overt display of 'lavatory necessities is offensive and against all sense of British decency']. (LCP Corr 1964/4604)

On both sides of the Atlantic, Beckett, as a theatrical neophyte, had become entangled not only in what seemed insurmountable negotiations with the Lord Chamberlain's office concerning the West End production of the play; he was also embroiled in the parallel saga of the New York opening. He finally responded to Rosset's alarm of potential rewriting of the American text in February 1956, thus just after the failure of Schneider's *Waiting for*

---

[23] Many of the Lord Chamberlain's documents are now available on the British Library's web page, including a response to Lady Hewitt's objections by N. W. Gwatkin: www.bl.uk/collection-items/lord-chamberlains-report-and-correspondence-about-waiting-for-godot. See also Flood (2017).

Godot in Miami, while the Criterion production was still running
(September 1955 to 24 March 1956), and the play's Broadway premiere
with its new director, Herbert Berghof in the offing (opening 19 April and
running until 9 June 1956):

> I am naturally disturbed by the thought of a new director of production [since he
> had no contact with Berghof]. And still more disturbed by the menace hinted at in
> one of your letters, of unauthorized deviations from the script. This we cannot
> have at any price and I am asking Albery to write Myerberg to that effect. I am
> not intransigent, as the [Bowdlerised] Criterion production shows, about minor
> changes, if I feel they are necessary, but I refuse to be improved by a professional
> rewriter. Perhaps it is a false alarm. I do hope so. (Beckett, 2011, 600–1)

It was not. Beckett's warning was both late and perhaps misplaced, uninformed
at least, since a revised text had already opened and closed in Miami and all the
pertinent decision had already been taken by Myerberg and Berghof to reverse the
Miami strategy and to stage Beckett's play at least with a mostly unaltered text.
Aside from a persistent naïveté about the workings of Anglo-American commercial
theatre into which he had plunged headlong, Beckett seems not to have realised,
since he was mostly kept in the dark through the process, that he had already been
substantially 'improved by a professional rewriter' and a pair of theatrical directors
by January 1956 but also that such 'improvements', authorised or not, were
routinely made for 'theatrical', that is, commercial reasons, and especially for
neophyte playwrights. It was the Bowdlerised version of *Godot* to which Beckett
alluded in the above quote that Faber & Faber finally published, to his displeasure,
even as the dossier from the Lord Chamberlain's office was restricted to public
performance and so had little sway over publication per se except as performance
might follow publication. That is, Faber & Faber resisted publishing a dramatic text
that could not be legally performed, or redirecting producers to a text that could be
performed, the *Samuel French 'Acting Edition'*. The censored British publication
by Faber & Faber seems to have been determined by such pre-emptive business
decisions but which the venerable house of Faber & Faber seems to have regretted
soon after, at least to Beckett. Writing to their author on 29 January 1957, Monteith
tried to offer Beckett some consolation: 'I would like to say, too, how unhappy
I feel, in retrospect, about our decision last year to print the Lord Chamberlain's
version of *Godot* rather than the full one', a decision he called 'perhaps an extreme
and undue timidity'. He further offered 'a faint plea in mitigation. I would like to
assure you, though, of our very sincere regrets that it should ever have happened'
(qtd in Faber, 2019, 243–4). But, in fact, Faber & Faber repeated its 'timidity' when
it prepared the 'paper covered' version of *Waiting for Godot* for publication, with

a copyright date of 1959 ('First published in this edition MCMLIX'),[24] the timidity repeated yet again in its 1962 reprint, 'Reprinted MCMLXII'.

The Lord Chamberlain's files for the play (LCP 1964/51) include this uncensored but mimeographed English State Company script that includes the Faber & Faber copyright dates of 1959 and 1962. This is the only rendering of what might have been – an uncensored, complete text published in 1959. On 2 June 2019, I wrote to the editors at Faber & Faber to enquire about these publications. I heard back as follows: 'The archivist has replied, "A fascinating query, Lavinia [Singer], and I will be happy to investigate for clues; but I am confident there is no surviving *Godot* typescript in the Faber archive"'. That observation was confirmed in a subsequent email: 'There are no *Godot* proofs in the archive, Lavinia. At that time they were not kept, but occasionally staff took them home, and they were later sold, etc.' Astonished at the reply, I queried yet again on 11 June, 'Presumably, s/he looked as well for a 1959 proof that was never fully published, at least until 1965 and then with different copyright dates', and that follow-up query was confirmed. A copy of the 'Uncorrected Proof' of the 1956 censored edition 'Proof Copy in paper wrappers', however, is on deposit at the Harry Ransom Center Book Collection, University of Texas; another is at the National Library of Ireland with 'Title inked on spine'; and one is in private hands, in the collection of Yuri Pattison, whose copy is attributable to the Faber editor Alan Pringle as 'Mr. Pringle' is pencilled on its paper cover. As of this writing, these are the only proof copies of the 1956 British *Godot* known to exist, and the Pattison copy is the only one with an annotation. As Pattison notes in an email to the author:

> My copy has one correction to the *characters* page, adding the omitted *Pozzo* in red biro with an arrow to the location of that name on the Grove copy (2nd from the bottom) but not the location actually used in the final Faber first edition (3rd from the bottom).

The meticulous printing on the Pattison proof copy looks remarkably like it could have been corrected by Beckett himself. Its placement in the list of characters, with a carefully drawn arrow, is not that of the final Faber & Faber publication, however, but that of the 1954 Grove Press edition. That is, Faber & Faber did not follow the placement of the correction in the proof copy as Beckett indicated but entered Pozzo in the list of characters before Lucky, thus in the order of their first lines in the play.

Further changes inevitably occurred when *Waiting for Godot* toured what David Kynaston has called 'the sticks' (Kynaston, 2010, 644) after the Criterion closing (24 March 1956). *Godot* returned to London on 2 July, opening at the

---

[24] The Monteith letter appears in excerpt in *Faber & Faber: The Untold Story*, edited by Toby Faber, but Monteith's second round of timidity remains an *Untold Story*, at least in that volume.

Golder's Green Hippodrome.[25] Initially, most of the actors of the touring production remained those of the Arts (3 August 1955) and Criterion (12 September 1955) productions, with the exception of Rob Eddison replacing Richard Dare as Vladimir and Derek Hodgson replacing Michael Walker as A Boy. Of more consequence is that the producing company for the tour was now Michael Wade and Richard Scott, Ltd, and not Independent Plays, Ltd, with Scott now credited as director rather than Peter Hall. The production designer, moreover, the one credited with 'Setting', was no longer Peter Snow but Jean Love, as the Golder's Green programme acknowledges. Sets are often simplified for touring troupes, and this change of 'Setting' designer likely afforded the opportunity to reduce the clutter of Snow's Arts and Criterion sets, which Beckett loathed.

6 The Case for Multiple Authorship

While all theatrical performance is subject to variation – from show to show, from theatre space to theatre space, from night to night, from actor to replacement actor – so that, as we acknowledged in Section 2, all performance is adaptation, to one degree or another, but the degree of variation, the differences between the contingencies of performance, and the deliberate reconfiguration of a text and its staging are the issues at play here. The production of *Waiting for Godot* that appeared on stage in Coral Gables, Florida, in January of 1956 was, unquestionably, a co-authored text, as were, to a lesser degree, the London premieres at both the Arts (August 1955) and Criterion theatres (September 1955 to March 1956) and the Dublin premiere at the Pike Theatre (October 1955), the director of each production tampering with or intervening in the text far beyond what the author would deem acceptable. Both credited (the Lord Chamberlain in the United Kingdom) and uncredited interventionists (producers and directors on both sides of the Atlantic) shaped the final performed texts but also some of what was subsequently published. Until the appearance of the 1965 restored and newly revised text of the play from Faber & Faber, the 1954 Grove Press edition was unique in being the only edition of

---

[25] The company began its provincial tour in late May but returned to London's Golder's Green Hippodrome on 2 July 1956 with mostly the London cast, then went on to the Birmingham Repertory Theatre (9 July 1956), the Royal Lyceum Theatre in Edinburgh (23 July 1956, for one week), the Opera House, Manchester (6 August 1956), and Leeds Grand (30 August 1956). The touring production also had a series of cast changes, often including Harold Lang, Michael Hichman, Edward Caddick, and Michael Peak. For more details and a fuller list of tour venues, see McMullan et al. (2014, 11–33); for more details on the 'varying interrelated cast' (15) of the touring productions, see McMullan et al. (2014, 30n5). David Kynaston lists the tour schedule, in addition to Blackpool, which he discusses at length, as follows: 'a provincial run, with original cast, that included weeks at Harrow, Cambridge, Bournemouth, Streatham [...] Golders Green and Birmingham' (Kynaston, 2010, 644).

Beckett's most famous play not rewritten, corrected, or improved, overtly or clandestinely, by other hands, even, as reported by Rosset to Beckett, Faber & Faber purchased the rights to that unaltered edition of the play by 24 September 1955, soon after the Criterion production had opened: 'Rosica Colin [of Curtis Brown] asked me if I would sell my translation rights for England for *Godot* to Faber for £ 50 and I said yes' (Rosset, 2017, 87). That sale was confirmed by 12 April 1956 as Rosset gave Beckett an economic update: 'We also sold the translation to Faber for $150, $75 of which is due to you' (see SULSC, Box 104). Faber & Faber flirted with publishing it but, finally, did not. The issue for the British publisher's hesitancy was public performance. Even if it had published the uncensored Grove Press edition, as Beckett advised and Rosset agreed, that version could not be staged in the United Kingdom given the restrictions still in place from the Lord Chamberlain's office, but those restrictions pertained in 1965 as well when Faber & Faber finally did publish its uncensored text. That is, those Lord Chamberlain restrictions were reaffirmed for the English Stage Company's attempt to stage an uncensored revival at the Royal Court Theatre in December of 1964 in anticipation, it was hoped, of Faber & Faber's publishing Beckett's full text, which did appear in 1965 as a 'second edition' in its 'paper covered editions' and in hard cover. The Grove Press text would remain, then, the only uncorrupted version of the play in print for a decade. Even after the appearance of the full text in 1965, however, all corrupted or censored versions of the published play did not vanish overnight. Publishers and booksellers continued to sell warehoused earlier editions, and corrupted texts continue to circulate in the aftermarket. Astoundingly, for its celebratory collection of Beckett's plays in 1986, Faber & Faber reprinted its sanitised 1956 edition (but continued to credit an unpublished 1955 performance edition that Samuel French also cites) of *Waiting for Godot* in *Samuel Beckett: The Complete Dramatic Works*,[26] a collection that never was, we hasten to add, 'Complete', and which was decorated in what may arguably be a contender for the ugliest book jacket ever designed. That publishing blunder was corrected, finally, but only in the 1990 paperback issue, even as the unsightly cover was retained. A second copyright date was added in 1990 to signal a change of *Godot* text to Faber & Faber's revised 1965 edition.

The 1955 copyright date cited in *The Complete Dramatic Works* is intriguing since it suggests that the choice of which *Godot* text to reissue may have been more deliberate than inadvertent, Faber & Faber editors thinking, perhaps, to publish the text as it was performed in the United Kingdom in that year, which,

---

[26] Another 'Bad *Godot*' was avoided as Grove Press declined to published this 'Complete' edition and thus did not repeat the Faber & Faber blunder.

finally, it was not. Closer to that performed text is the *Samuel French 'Acting Edition'*, a distorted, co-authored text that was not replaced until 2004, nearly forty years after the Faber & Faber revised text appeared in 1965, and those pre-2004 editions, likewise, remain stockpiled in school theatre department closets and libraries, where they awaited their day – to be taught, studied, and performed yet again. Federman and Fletcher in their landmark 1970 bibliography already refer to the *Samuel French 'Acting Edition'* as one prepared by 'adapters': 'It must be said that the adapters have tampered extensively and naively with dialogue and stage directions', although they incorrectly identify the Miami production as 'directed by Michael Myerberg' (Federman and Fletcher, 1970, 78). Van Hulle and Verhulst note of the play's 'adapters' that 'Who they were is not revealed, but Peter Hall and Peter Snow, the director and the set designer of the London Criterion production, are likely candidates' (Van Hulle and Verhulst, 2018, 119). Asked directly by John Fletcher if he had authorised such an edition, Beckett responded on 6 July 1966 that he had 'no recollection of the Samuel French thing' and that he 'cannot have accepted such an edition' (qtd in Van Hulle and Verhulst, 2018, 119), although clearly his American publisher had authorised it.

Given the breadth of its distribution and its longevity, the dearth of critical and performance-related commentary on this widely distributed *Samuel French 'Acting Edition'* is nothing short of astonishing, almost nothing between Federman and Fletcher (1970) and Van Hulle and Verhulst (2018) – and this includes the otherwise exemplary volume of 2017, *Staging Beckett in Great Britain* – but even Van Hulle and Verhulst do not deem this edition significant enough for inclusion in their 'Genetic Map' (Van Hulle and Verhulst, 2018, 164). No mention is made of the Samuel French text, moreover, in Sos Eltis' essay, '"It's All Symbiosis": Peter Hall Directing Beckett', where Eltis celebrates the director 'As a great respecter of Beckett's words' (Eltis, 2016, 88). 'Hall is scrupulous in following Beckett's text exactly', she adds, with the added qualifications that 'his attitude toward the minutiae of Beckett's stage business is more relaxed' and that 'Hall has been content on occasion to diverge explicitly from Beckett's staging' (Eltis, 2016, 89). Such celebration of Hall's textual fidelity, even if restricted to 'Beckett's words', is possible only by bracketing or otherwise avoiding the textual rewritings of both 1955 London productions and focusing on Hall's subsequent work: *Happy Days* (at the Old Vic in 1975 and the Lyttleton in 1976, with a script revised by Beckett, and the 2003 revival) and his *Godot* revivals (1997 and the fiftieth anniversary production in 2005). For these, Hall indeed paid studious attention to Beckett's revised script for *Happy Days* and to the textual alterations in the *Godot* volume of *The Theatrical Notebooks of Samuel Beckett* among other archived production documents, as Eltis details. Curiously, Eltis also cites Hall's quip denigrating Alan Schneider's purported textual fealty: 'His fidelity can verge on the mechanical and his productions were sometimes more accurate than inspired' (Hall qtd in Eltis, 2016, 89). Eltis mentions neither Hall's rewrites for the English-language premieres of *Godot* nor their permanent record in the *Samuel French 'Acting Edition'* of the play.

Furthermore, the *Waiting for Godot* texts cited in the *Staging Beckett in Great Britain*'s bibliography are, at best, quirky and further suggest unresolved gaps early and late in the play's transmission, publication, and performance history. The only stand-alone edition of *Waiting for Godot* acknowledged in *Staging Beckett in Great Britain* (2016) – beyond the *Theatrical Notebook*, Volume I and *The Complete Dramatic Works*, listed thrice in two different formats (1986, 1990, 2006) – is a Faber reprint of 2006. Faber & Faber's uniform edition was available from 2010, however. Its 'Preface' reminds us that 'The journey through text, transmission and reception was [...] a long and complex one' (Bryden, 2010, vii) but without specifics, and no mention is made of the *Samuel French 'Acting Edition'* as part of that transmission complexity. On the other hand, the *Krapp's Last Tape and Other Shorter Plays* volume of 2009 in the same series originally referred to what Beckett called 'the Samuel French thing' in 'Some Notes on Texts and Textuality' as follows: 'An acting edition of *Godot*, with details of the first production, a stage diagram, properties and lighting effects, was published in London by Samuel French (Acting Editions #510) in 1957 with significant variants from either Grove or Faber editions'. That sentence was excised from the published version by Faber & Faber house editors shortly before printing, however. For the historical record, readers can go to the 'Unmutilated "Preface"' for that Faber & Faber volume that was subsequently published as 'Appendix I' to 'A Centenary of Missed Opportunities: Assembling an Accurate Volume of Samuel Beckett's Dramatic "Shorts"' (Gontarski, 2011, 374–82). Furthermore, we might stress again that another significant feature of this textual and production overview is to reemphasise the attempt in 1964 by the Royal Court Theatre to stage an uncensored production of *Godot*, directed by Anthony Page under Beckett supervision, which was finally thwarted by the Lord Chamberlain's office. Surprisingly, that historic attempt to break through the United Kingdom's formal censorship practices goes unmentioned in *Staging Beckett in Great Britain*, with the director Anthony Page referred to only once in the volume and that in another context, in my own essay on *Endgame*.

The first Dublin staging was likewise based on a rewritten script, or at least one substantially localised. Nicholas Grene notes that his 'examination of the promptbook used by [Alan] Simpson for this [Pike Theatre] production reveals that the text was systematically "Hibernicized", with many phrases re-written in a colloquial Irish English' (Grene, 2008, 135). When Christopher Murray characterises the Dublin premiere in *Staging Beckett in Ireland and Northern Ireland* (2016), he notes that 'Simpson is the paradigmatic director in this regard: he was determined to give to this play a local habitation and lilt', and, he continues, 'Beckett regarded such a procedure as tampering with the "integrity" of his play. Today it would more likely be seen as collaboration between a novice playwright and an astute instinctive director' (Murray, 2016, xvi). Murray's justification for such overt rewriting relies on a cultural shift, a change of attitudes towards theatrical collaborations in our day. In parallel to Murray's emphasis on cultural shift by the 1960s, we can add that the censorship function of the Lord Chamberlain's office was eliminated by the Theatres Act of 1968, the year in which Beckett takes on acknowledged direction of his own plays.

Many of the issues discussed herein, of textual intervention and tampering, of adaptation, of rewriting, of multiple or co-authorship, take a more theoretical turn once the originating author is involved, however. By 1968, such issues of textual integrity gain further complications when Beckett begins to look back over his own theatrical output and to approach it as something like, after Roland Barthes, say, *Samuel Beckett by Samuel Beckett*, as he began to stage, that is, to realise his own scripts and thereby to become his own collaborator as he embodied his work and rendered it into spatial form. This was a Barthesian encounter, a writer critiquing his own creative production, and its record, Beckett's having become his own interventionist or co-author, appears in four volumes of *The Theatrical Notebooks of Samuel Beckett* published between 1992 and 1999 and subsequently in more accessible, affordable paperback editions between 2019 and 2021, and they detail not so much a continuation of an authorial process but a fresh intervention by another, and so his stagings might be seen as co-authored texts as well, a realisation on stage and now in print, by another, a new collaborator in the theatrical process, one named Samuel Beckett. The tenuousness and uncertainty of that theatrical relationship – this tale of two Becketts, at least – have meant that while Beckett established new, leaner, clearer acting texts through that process, and these have been published, now reissued in 2019–21 – and used in performance by major directors like Peter Hall and Katie Mitchell – they have yet to appear separately as what they are, either 'Acting Editions' or 'Final Texts' and thus in competition with or to offset the Samuel French publications.

Scripts specified as 'Acting Editions' remain popular for their handy, soft cover format that actors and directors can hold, annotate, fold, and otherwise manipulate, and they retain a certain priority by that designation, and so the *Samuel French 'Acting Edition'* of 1957 was in economic (at least) competition (at 6s) with the Faber & Faber hardback (at 10s 6d) – at least until the 1965 paperback (also now at 6s or 'GBP 0.30 net', but with 'a clothbound edition priced at 16s net').[27] Those competing British editions also punctuate the curious nature of this genre, theatre, as printed text may differ, and at times substantially so, from what appears on stage. The Signet paperback edition of Tennessee Williams' *Cat on a Hot Tin Roof*, for example, contains two third acts, the one written by Tennessee Williams and the one rewritten in production by the director Elia Kazan and actually performed on Broadway. Such texts might be deemed collaborative or multi-authored, as the third act of *Cat on a Hot Tin Roof* indeed was. In Beckett's case, we might ask who, finally, wrote the script for the *Waiting for Godot* we are reading, or who 'authored' the performance we are watching? The answer may depend on what one means by such a question, which edition one is holding, say, or how much attention the producer and director (at least) have paid to the script they at least began with before other theatrical collaborators – producers, directors, actors, and invest- ors – entered the scene. As previously noted, even if they are corrupted, overtly rewritten texts remain part of the marketplace. They are seldom withdrawn for reasons of infidelity and so remain in circulation.

Textual alterations may be minor on the whole, but they are almost never inconsequential. 'French's' or *Samuel French 'Acting Edition'* is the high-water mark of textual intervention even as it has attracted little attention from Beckett scholars. Minor as each rewriting may be individually, the range of these alterations is vast as Beckett's terse, astringent prose is continually inflated, the silences rendered less so, the sparse, arid set littered with a tar barrel, cattails, hanging vines, 'A rostrum', and other cluttering 'details' – and Pozzo's whip-wielding cruelty is diminished. If, moreover, as strangers approach, '*They huddle together, behind the barrel*' (Beckett, 1957, 10); if, as Vladimir remembers, 'The mother embroidered d'oylies' (12); if Pozzo 'took a stooge' (21); if Beckett's 'even a shilling' (i.e., 12 pence) (Beckett, 1956, 38) is rendered into street slang, 'even a bob' (Beckett, 1957, 25–6); if '*Estragon is fiddling with his boot again*' (Beckett, 1956, 37) becomes '*Estragon crosses, sits on the barrel, and fiddles with his boot*', and the subsequent exchange about Pozzo's whip and Estragon's name disappear (Beckett, 1957, 24); and if, to open Act II, '*Vladimir emerges from the barrel, and stands erect*' (39), whom do we credit with authorship? Beckett's very simple end to Lucky's speech, '*(melee, final vociferations)*' (Beckett, 1954, 29b; Albery I-41) is re-rendered as follows: '*(There is a general* mêlée. *VLADIMIR and ESTRAGON protest violently. POZZO jumps up and pulls on the rope. There is a general outcry. ESTRAGON moves to R of LUCKY and seizes him. VLADIMIR moves to L of*

---

27   The Net Book Agreement (NBA) of 1899 established set book prices between the UK Publishers Association and booksellers. This price-fixing agreement remained in effect until 1997.

Lucky)' / '– (*he [Pozzo] pulls on the rope, staggers and shouts*' (Beckett, 1957, 30). And visually, the setting suggested in the *Samuel French 'Acting Edition'* is lushly un-Beckettian. As the University of Reading teaching blog has it: 'Hall's Arts Theatre production featured a rather bog like set with reeds and thick undergrowth' (McMullan, 2017). That same cluttered set was used for the Criterion production as well (see *Theatre Arts*, Beckett, 1956c, 41–2, 45, 49, 55, 57 for photos), doubtless simplified by the new designer, Jean Love, for the subsequent touring production. It is not too far a stretch to imagine, moreover, a similar expansive scenario having played out in Miami, and subsequently in New York had what we have been calling Schneider's Wilderised Beckett remained in play. Such a prospect was forestalled in the United States, finally, as the revised genealogy of the American premiere of Beckett's first produced play offered in this Element, particularly in Section 2, suggests, by an abrupt change both of director and in direction as Myerberg, then, belatedly, Schneider, would follow Rosset, the only figure in this early period of performances of *Waiting for Godot* in English firmly committed to Beckett's authorial integrity. The Miami rewritings, unlike those in the United Kingdom, however, never achieved the permanence of publication, and so the production remained, like that at Dublin's Pike Theatre, a local and localised adaptation. On the other hand, at least six 'bad *Godots*' under discussion here have been enshrined in print: three published or generated by Faber & Faber (1956, reprinted in Suhrkamp's trilingual *Dramatische Dichtungen* of 1963 and in Faber & Faber edition of 1986) and three, including the *Samuel French 'Acting Edition'*, were authorised by Grove Press, which controlled world performance rights in English.

Bibliography

Atkinson, Brooks (1956), 'Beckett's "Waiting for Godot"', *New York Times*, 20 April. https://archive.nytimes.com/www.nytimes.com/books/97/08/03/reviews/beckett-godot.html?module=inline

Barnes, Clive (1976), 'Theater: Brilliant Fragments of Beckett', *New York Times*, 10 December, 64. www.nytimes.com/1976/12/10/archives/theater-brilliant-fragments-of-beckett.html

Barney Rosset Papers; Rare Book and Manuscript Library, Columbia University Library. https://findingaids.library.columbia.edu/ead/nnc-rb/ldpd_7953908/dsc/6#subseries_1

Beckett–Rosset Correspondence: Typed draft 2, undated, folder 1, box 10, Stanley E. Gontarski Grove Press Research Materials, MSS 2013-0516. FSU Special Collections & Archives. https://archives.lib.fsu.edu/repositories/10/archival_objects/144205

Beckett, Samuel (1953a), *Waiting for Godot*, Mimeograph, cover numbered in pen, 15, Harry Ransom Humanities Research Center, the University of Texas at Austin.

Beckett, Samuel (1953b), *Waiting for Godot*, Mimeograph, unnumbered copy, BDMP MS-HRC-DA-145-1 and Harry Ransom Humanities Research Center, the University of Texas at Austin.

Beckett, Samuel (1953c), *Waiting for Godot*, Mimeograph, cover numbered in pen, 25, Harry Ransom Humanities Research Center, the University of Texas at Austin.

Beckett, Samuel (1953d), *Waiting for Godot*, Mimeograph, cover unnumbered. Cited as Ohio State University, Columbus, Ohio.

Beckett, Samuel (1953/4), *Waiting for Godot*, Lord Chamberlain Plays LCP 1954/23, Mimeograph, cover numbered in red pen, 12. BDMP MS-BL-LCP-1954-23. British Library, London. [Mimeograph of Beckett's first (1953) translation with the Lord Chamberlain's proposed cuts marked in red.]. Cover and two images available at: www.bl.uk/collection-items/censored-script-of-waiting-for-godot-by-samuel-beckett

Beckett, Samuel (1954), *Waiting for Godot*, New York: Grove Press.

Beckett, Samuel (1956a), *Waiting for Godot*, London: Faber & Faber.

Beckett, Samuel (1956b), *Waiting for Godot, The Best Plays, 1955–56*, ed. Louis Kronenberger, New York: Dodd, Mead & Company, pp. 295–317.

Beckett, Samuel (1956c), *Waiting for Godot, Theatre Arts*, 40:8 (August), pp. 36–61.

Beckett, Samuel (1957), *Waiting for Godot*, London: Samuel French.

Beckett, Samuel (1964), *Waiting for Godot*, Lord Chamberlain Plays LCP 1964/ 51, British Library, London [Retyped mimeograph copy submitted.].

Beckett, Samuel (1965a), *Waiting for Godot*, London: Faber & Faber.

Beckett, Samuel (1965b), *Waiting for Godot*, Lord Chamberlain Plays LCP 1965/47. British Library, London.

Beckett, Samuel (1986), *The Complete Dramatic Works*, London: Faber & Faber.

Beckett, Samuel (1992), *The Theatrical Notebooks of Samuel Beckett, Vol. II: 'Endgame'*, ed. S. E. Gontarski, London: Faber & Faber.

Beckett, Samuel (1992), *The Theatrical Notebooks of Samuel Beckett, Vol. III: 'Krapp's Last Tape'*, ed. James Knowlson, London: Faber & Faber; New York: Grove Press.

Beckett, Samuel (1994), *The Theatrical Notebooks of Samuel Beckett, Vol. I: 'Waiting for Godot'*, ed. James Knowlson, London: Faber & Faber; New York: Grove Press.

Beckett, Samuel (1999), *The Theatrical Notebooks of Samuel Beckett, Vol. IV: The Shorter Plays*, ed. S. E. Gontarski, London: Faber & Faber; New York: Grove Press.

Beckett, Samuel (2009), *The Letters of Samuel Beckett, Vol. I: 1929–1940*, ed. Martha Dow Fehsenfeld and Lois More Overbeck, Cambridge: Cambridge University Press.

Beckett, Samuel (2010), *Waiting for Godot*, 'Preface' by Mary Bryden, London: Faber & Faber.

Beckett, Samuel (2011), *The Letters of Samuel Beckett, Vol. II: 1941–1956*, ed. George Craig, Martha Dow Fehsenfeld, Dan Gunn, and Lois More Overbeck, Cambridge: Cambridge University Press.

Beckett, Samuel (2014), *The Letters of Samuel Beckett, Vol. III: 1957–1965*, ed. George Craig, Martha Dow Fehsenfeld, Dan Gunn, and Lois More Overbeck, Cambridge: Cambridge University Press.

Beckett, Samuel and Alan Schneider (1998), *'No Author Better Served': The Correspondence of Samuel Beckett and Alan Schneider*, ed. Maurice Harmon, Cambridge, MA: Harvard University Press.

Beckett, Samuel and Richard Scott (1956), *Michael Wide and Richard Scott Ltd. Present Samuel Beckett's Priceless, Inimitable Waiting for Godot [Playbill]: The Most Discussed Play in London: Following Its Success at the Criterion Theatre*. [Edinburgh: Royal Lyceum Theatre].

Bianchini, Natka (2015), *Samuel Beckett's Theatre in America: The Legacy of Alan Schneider As Beckett American Director*, New York: Palgrave Macmillan.

Bryden, Mary (2010), 'Preface', in Samuel Beckett, *Waiting for Godot*, London: Faber & Faber, pp. vii–xiii.

Campbell, Joseph (2003), *Mythic Worlds, Modern Words: On the Art of James Joyce*, ed. Edward L. Epstein, Novato, CA: New World Library, pp. 257–66.

Cronin, Anthony (1997), *Beckett: The Last Modernist*, London: HarperCollins Publishers.

Dukes, Gerry (1995a), 'The Pike Theatre Typescript of *Waiting for Godot*: Part I', *Journal of Beckett Studies*, 4:2 (spring), pp. 77–92.

Dukes, Gerry (1995b), 'Beckett's Synge-Song: The Revised *Godot* Revisited', *Journal of Beckett Studies*, 4:2 (spring), pp. 103–12.

Eltis, Sos (2016), '"It's All Symbiosis": Peter Hall Directing Beckett', in David Tucker and Trish McTigue (eds), *Staging Beckett in Great Britain*, London: Bloomsbury Methuen Drama, pp. 87–106.

Faber, Toby (2019), *Faber & Faber: The Untold Story*, London: Faber & Faber.

Federman, Raymond and John Fletcher, eds (1970), *Samuel Beckett: His Works and His Critics*, Berkeley, CA: University of California Press.

Flood, Allison (2017), '"Angry Boredom": Early Responses to *Waiting for Godot* Showcased Online', *The Guardian*, September 11. www.theguardian.com/books/2017/sep/11/early-responses-to-waiting-for-godot-showcased-online-samuel-beckett

Gontarski, S. E., ed. (1990), *Grove Press Number: The Review of Contemporary Fiction*, 10:3 (fall).

Gontarski, S. E. (1999), 'Bowdlerizing Beckett: The BBC Embers', *Journal of Beckett Studies*, 9.1 (fall), pp. 127–132.

Gontarski, S. E. (2011), 'A Centenary of Missed Opportunities: Assembling an Accurate Volume of Samuel Beckett's Dramatic "Shorts"', *Modern Drama*, 54:3 (fall), pp. 357–82.

Gontarski, S. E. (2018), 'Ballocksed, Banjaxed or Banjoed: Textual Aberrations, Ghost Texts, and the British *Godot*', *Journal of Modern Literature*, 41:4, pp. 48–67. https://doi.org/10.2979/jmodelite.41.4.04

Grene, Nicholas (2008), 'The Hibernicization of *En Attendant Godot*', *Études irlandaises*, 33:2, Théâtres de France et d'Irlande: influences et interactions, sous la direction de Martine Pelletier et Alexandra Poulain, pp. 135–44. https://doi.org/10.3406/irlan.2008.1844

Grove Press Records, Special Collections Research Center, Syracuse University Libraries, cited as SULSC. The Beckett–Rosset correspondence on *Waiting for Godot* of this period is available in Box 104, *Waiting for Godot*, 'Correspondence 1953–1969'.

Gussow, Mel (1988), 'The Darker Shore of Thornton Wilder', *New York Times*, 11 December: sec. 2:7. www.nytimes.com/1988/12/11/theater/theater-view-the-darker-shores-of-thornton-wilder.html

Hall, Peter (2005), 'Godot Almighty', *The Guardian*, 24 August. www.theguardian.com/stage/2005/aug/24/theatre.beckettat100

Harrison, Gilbert A. (1983), *The Enthusiast: A Life of Thornton Wilder*, New York: Ticknor and Fields.

Knowlson, James (1996), *Damned to Fame: The Life of Samuel Beckett*, New York: Simon & Schuster.

Kronenberger, Louis, ed. (1956), *The Best Plays, 1955–56*, New York: Dodd, Mead & Company.

Kynaston, David (2010), *Family Britain, 1951–1957* (Tales of a New Jerusalem series), London: Bloomsbury Publishing.

Lahr, John (2009), 'Panic Attack: *Waiting for Godot* Back on Broadway', *New Yorker*, 11 May. www.newyorker.com/magazine/2009/05/18/panic-attack

Levy, Alan (1956), 'the LONG wait for godot' [*sic*], *Theatre Arts*, 40:8 (August), pp. 33–5, 96.

'Lord Chamberlain's Report and Correspondence about *Waiting for Godot*', British Library: www.bl.uk/collection-items/lord-chamberlains-report-and-correspondence-about-waiting-for-godot. (See also Flood, 2017.)

Lord Chamberlain Plays Correspondence, LCP Corr 1954/6597, LCP Corr 1964/4604, and LCP Corr 1965/304, British Library, London. www.bl.uk/collection-items/censored-script-of-waiting-for-godot-by-samuel-beckett

Lord Chamberlain Plays LCP 1954/23, LCP 1964/51, and LCP 1965/47, British Library, London.

McMullan, Anna (2017), 'Sir Peter Hall's Encounters with *Godot*', Connecting Research: The Forum (blog), University of Reading, 18 September. https://blogs.reading.ac.uk/the-forum/2017/09/18/sir-peter-halls-encounters-with-godot/

McMullan, Anna, Trish McTighe, David Pattie, and David Tucker (2014), 'Staging Beckett: Constructing Histories of Performance', *Journal of Beckett Studies*, 23:1 (April), pp. 11–33.

McTigue, Trish and David Tucker, eds (2016), *Staging Beckett in Ireland and Northern Ireland*, London: Bloomsbury Methuen Drama.

Martin, Stewart (2007), 'The Absolute Artwork Meets the Absolute Commodity', *Radical Philosophy*, 146:15, pp. 15–25. https://platypus1917.org/wp-content/uploads/2010/10/martinstewart_absoluteartworkcommodity_rp2007.pdf

Maxwell, Jane (2006), 'The Samuel Beckett Manuscripts at Trinity College Library Dublin', *Samuel Beckett Today/Aujourd'hui*, 16, pp. 183–99. www.jstor.org/stable/25781732

Murray, Christopher (1984), 'Beckett Productions in Ireland: A Survey', *Irish University Review*, 14:1, pp. 103–25. www.jstor.org/stable/25477527

Murray, Christopher (2016), 'Foreword', in Trish McTigue and David Tucker (eds), *Staging Beckett in Ireland and Northern Ireland*, London: Bloomsbury Methuen Drama, pp. xv–xxii.

Niven, Penelope (2012), *Thornton Wilder: A Life*, New York: Harper.

Rosset, Barney (1997), 'The Art of Publishing No.2', *Paris Review*, 145 (winter), pp. 299–331.

Rosset, Barney (2016), *Rosset: My Life in Publishing and How I Fought Censorship*, New York: O/R Books.

Rosset, Barney (2017), *Dear Mr. Beckett: The Samuel Beckett File*, ed. Lois Oppenheim, curated by Astrid Myers, Tuxedo Park, NY: Opus.

Schneider, Alan (1955), Prompt book, retyped copy of Grove Press published edition of *Waiting for Godot*, Alan Schneider Archive, Title 17, 107–8, University of California, San Diego.

Schneider, Alan (1971), 'No More Waiting', *New York Times*, January 31: sec. D, p. 1. www.nytimes.com/1971/01/31/archives/no-more-waiting-no-more-waiting.html

Schneider, Alan (1985), 'Waiting for Beckett', *New York Times*, November 17: sec. 6, p. 47.

Schneider, Alan (1986), *Entrances: An American Director's Journey*, London: Penguin.

'Stanley E. Gontarski Grove Press Research Materials': Beckett–Rosset Correspondence: Typed draft 2, undated, folder 1, box 10, Stanley E. Gontarski Grove Press Research Materials, MSS 2013-0516. FSU Special Collections & Archives. https://archives.lib.fsu.edu/repositories/10/archival_objects/144205

Suther, Jenson (2017), 'Black as the New Dissonance: Heidegger, Adorno and Truth in the Work of Art', *Mediations: Journal of the Marxist Literary Group*, 31:1, pp. 95–122 (Recombinations and Configurations). https://mediationsjournal.org/files/Mediations31_1.pdf

Swift, Carolyn (1996), 'Beckett Biographies', *Irish Times*, 11 October. www.irishtimes.com/opinion/letters/beckett-biographies-1.94737

Tallmer, Jerry (1956), '*Godot* on Broadway '56', *Village Voice*, April 25.

Tucker, David and Trish McTigue, eds (2016), *Staging Beckett in Great Britain*, London: Bloomsbury Methuen Drama.

Van Hulle, Dirk (2019), 'Beckett's Art of the Commonplace: The "Sottisier" Notebook and *mirlitonnades* Drafts', *The Journal of Beckett Studies*, 28:1, pp. 67–89.

Van Hulle, Dirk and Pim Verhulst (2018), *The Making of Samuel Beckett's 'En attendant Godot'/'Waiting for Godot'*, London: Bloomsbury.

Wilder, Robin and Jackson R. Bryer, eds (2008), *The Selected Letters of Thornton Wilder*, New York: HarperCollins Publishers.

Wilder, Thornton (1957), 'Preface', in *Three Plays*, New York: Harper and Brothers Publishers.

Wilson, Edmund (1943), 'The Antrobuses and the Earwickers', *Nation*, 30 January, pp. 167–8.

Wilson, Edmund (1950), *Classics and Commercials: A Literary Chronicle of the 1940s*, New York: Farrar, Straus and Giroux, pp. 61–6; also includes 'A Guide to *Finnegans Wake*', pp. 182–9, a review of Campbell and Robinson's *A Skeleton Key to 'Finnegans Wake'*, originally published 26 August 1944.

Cambridge Elements ≡

Beckett Studies

Dirk Van Hulle
University of Oxford

Dirk Van Hulle is Professor of Bibliography and Modern Book History at the University of Oxford and director of the Centre for Manuscript Genetics at the University of Antwerp.

Mark Nixon
University of Reading

Mark Nixon is Associate Professor in Modern Literature at the University of Reading and the Co-Director of the Beckett International Foundation.

About the Series

This series presents cutting-edge research by distinguished and emerging scholars, providing space for the most relevant debates informing Beckett studies as well as neglected aspects of his work. In times of technological development, religious radicalism, unprecedented migration, gender fluidity, environmental and social crisis, Beckett's works find increased resonance. Cambridge Elements in Beckett Studies is a key resource for readers interested in the current state of the field.

Cambridge Elements ≡

Beckett Studies

Elements in the Series

A full series listing is available at: www.cambridge.org/eibs

Printed in the United States
by Baker & Taylor Publisher Services